Kalidasa

Ṛtusaṁhāra
The Pageant of Seasons

Bengali translation and illustrations by
Asit Haldar

English translation by
Richard Hartz

Edited by
Debashish Banerji

The Pageant of Seasons
Copyright : Debashish Banerji
Bengali translation and illustrations by Asit Haldar
English translation by Richard Hartz
First edition 2023

ISBN 978-93-95460-76-7 (eBook)
ISBN 978-93-95460-51-4 (Print)

BISAC Code:
POE000000, POETRY / General
SOC002010, SOCIAL SCIENCE / Anthropology / Cultural & Social
SOC003000, SOCIAL SCIENCE / Archaeology
SOC015000, SOCIAL SCIENCE / Human Geography
NAT010000, NATURE / Ecology
LAN005070, LANGUAGE ARTS & DISCIPLINES / Writing / Poetry

Thema Subject Category:
2BMB, Bengali
2BBA, Sanskrit
5PB, Relating to peoples: ethnic groups, indigenous peoples, cultures and other groupings of people
5P, Relating to specific groups and cultures or social and cultural interests
DC , Poetry
YPJX, Educational: Cultural studies
RGCS, Social geography
GTM, Regional / International studies

Cataloging-in-Publication Data for this title is available from the Library of Congress.

PRISMA, an imprint of Digital Media Initiatives
PRISMA, Aurelec / Prayogshala,
Auroville 605101, Tamil Nadu, India
www.prisma.haus

The Pageant of Seasons
Copyright : Debashish Banerji
Bengali translation and illustrations by Asit Haldar
English translation by Richard Hartz
First edition 2023

ISBN 978-93-95460-76-7 (eBook)
ISBN 978-93-95460-51-4 (Print)

BISAC Code:
POE000000, POETRY / General
SOC002010, SOCIAL SCIENCE / Anthropology / Cultural & Social
SOC003000, SOCIAL SCIENCE / Archaeology
SOC015000, SOCIAL SCIENCE / Human Geography
NAT010000, NATURE / Ecology
LAN005070, LANGUAGE ARTS & DISCIPLINES / Writing / Poetry

Thema Subject Category:
2BMB, Bengali
2BBA, Sanskrit
5PB, Relating to peoples: ethnic groups, indigenous peoples, cultures and other groupings of people
5P, Relating to specific groups and cultures or social and cultural interests
DC , Poetry
YPJX, Educational: Cultural studies
RGCS, Social geography
GTM, Regional / International studies

Cataloging-in-Publication Data for this title is available from the Library of Congress.

PRISMA, an imprint of Digital Media Initiatives
PRISMA, Aurelec / Prayogshala,
Auroville 605101, Tamil Nadu, India
www.prisma.haus

Kalidasa

Ṛtusaṁhāra
The Pageant of Seasons

Bengali translation and illustrations by
Asit Haldar

English translation by
Richard Hartz

Edited by
Debashish Banerji

CONTENTS

Dedication (নিবেদন) *Asit Kumar Haldar*	7
Editor's Introduction *Debashish Banerji*	9
Introduction to *The Seasons* *Richard Hartz*	35
Note on the English Translation *Richard Hartz*	57
Canto 1: Summer	75
Canto 2: The Rains	109
Canto 3: Autumn	143
Canto 4: Winter	175
Canto 5: Dew-Time	199
Canto 6: Spring	221

নিবেদন

ঋতুসংহার কাব্যটিকে অনেকে মনে করেন মহাকবি কালিদাসের অপরিণত রচনা ; কেননা তাঁরা এটিতে অপর সকল কাব্যের মত 'উপমা তুলনা মন্ডিত মাধুর্য্য ও রূপকারের অলৌকিক ক্ষমতা', প্রকৃতি বর্ণন বিষয় পাননা। অপরিণত রচনা হলেও শিল্পী ও কবিদের নিকট ঋতুসংহার একটি অপূর্ব কাব্য সৃষ্টি । প্রকৃতি বর্ণনায় ঋতুবর্তনের খণ্ড খণ্ড বিচিত্র রূপগুলি তরু, লতা, জীব প্রভৃতির পরিকল্পনাকে অবলম্বন করে তুলনা ও উপমার দ্বারা কবি এমন সুন্দর ভাবে প্রকাশ করেছেন যে সকলকালের সকল কবি ও শিল্পীকে ইহা চিরদিনই অনুপ্রেরণা যোগাবে ।

কবি ও শিল্পীদের কাজই হ'ল অব্যক্তকে ব্যক্ত করা । মানুষ যা' এই জীবনে দেখেচ বা অনুভব করেচে তাকে স ধরে রাখতে পারচেনা, বা সকলের জন্যে পরিবেষণ করতে পারচেনা সকল সময় । কবি ও শিল্পীর কাজই হ'ল এই অনুভূতিকে সকলের জন্য এবং সকল কালের জন্য জাগরূক রাখা । চিত্র শিল্পীর পক্ষে যেমন পটের ক্ষুদ্র আয়তন, রেখা, রঙ ও তুলির-ক্ষমতা-সীমাকে স্বীকার করে নিতে হয়, তেমনি কবিকেও তাঁর ভাষার মধ্যে, শব্দের গণ্ডিকে ভুলিলে চলেনা। তাই দেখা যায় প্রত্যেক কবির শিক্ষা ও সংস্কার ভেদে রস-পরিবেষণের ভঙ্গী তাঁর নির্ব্বাচিত বিশেষ শব্দগুলিকে বহন করে চলে । এইরূপ শব্দ চয়নের স্বকীয়তার বিষয়ে কোনা তর্ক চলেনা । তেমনি আবার কবি মাত্রেই জানেন যে কাব্যকলাকে সম্পূর্ণ রূপে সংগত করতে গেলে অনেক সময় কাব্যের রস ও শব্দ বিন্যাসের সহজ ছন্দগতি খর্ব হয়—তার সাবলীল ভাবটি ক্ষুন্ন হয় । এই সকল কারণেই মহাকবি ভাস ও কালিদাসের মত ব্যক্তিরা শোনা যায় কূটনীতিজ্ঞ পণ্ডিতদের হাত থেকে দূর থাকতে চাইতেন । কাব্যের মধ্যে যে ভাষার অসম্পূর্ণতাকে বহন করে অব্যক্ত অপরূপ একটি অনুভূতি ফুটে ওঠে সেইটিই কাব্যকলার প্রাণ এবং তাহাই কাব্যরসিকের ও শিল্পীদের মনে ছবির পরিকল্পনা ও অনুরণন এনে দেয় । এই অভিজ্ঞতা শিল্পী ও কাব্যরসিক মাত্রেই জীবনে লাভ করার সুযোগ পান কাব্যপাঠে এবং কাব্যের সার্থকতা এইখানেই স্পষ্ট সূচিত হয় ।

ঋতুসংহারে কবি প্রকৃতিবর্ণনাকালে যে রস পরিবেষণ করেছেন তা সকল শিল্পীর পক্ষেই তাই এত আদরণীয় । সংজ্ঞাবোধ (intuition) যেমন সঙ্গীতের পক্ষে, অনুবোধ (sensation) যেমন নক্সাকারী পরিকল্পনার (design-এর) পক্ষে, অনুমান (hypothesis) যেমন বিজ্ঞানের (science-এর) পক্ষে, তেমনি অনুভূতি (feeling) কাব্যকলার পক্ষে প্রাণস্বরূপ । অতএব বৈয়াকরণিকের চুলচিরে অঙ্গবিভাগ দ্বারা পরীক্ষার স্থান কাব্যে নাই । এই অনুভূতির (feeling-এর) স্বচ্ছ যবনিকার মধ্যে কবি ও শিল্পী প্রকৃতির রূপবৈচিত্র্যের পূর্ণ পরিচয় পান সাধনার দ্বারা এবং তাই তাঁদের পরস্পরকে চিনতে বা জানতে বিলম্ব হয়না । কবি ও শিল্পীর এই সাধনা সময়-বিনোদনের অকারণ আনন্দসম্ভূত, এতে আহার সংস্থানের জন্য করা কাজের মত পরিশ্রমের চিহ্ন মাত্র নেই । আনন্দ-অনুভূতির বিকাশই এর প্রকৃতি ।

বাঙলা ভাষায় এই কাব্যটির পদ্যানুবাদ নামকরা কোনো কবি এপর্য্যন্ত করেছেন কিনা তা' জানা

নেই । বোধহয় রুচি-বিরুদ্ধ হওয়ায় কবিরা তর্জ্জমা করতে বিরত হয়েচেন । অবশ্য আধুনিক রুচি যতই মার্জ্জিত হোক কবি আধ্যাত্মিক জগতের যে নয়—পরিনির্ব্বাণের পথে যে তাঁর পরিসমাপ্তি নয়, একথা বলাই বাহুল্য । সৃষ্টিতত্ত্বের দিক দিয়ে দেখলে সকল সৃষ্টির প্রকাশ ভঙ্গীতে যা' আদি রসরূপ বর্ত্তমান আছে তাহাই প্রাচীন কাব্যে চলতো, তা' এখন আর চলেনা । অতএব আধুনিক রুচি অনুসারে সেই সকল অংশের তীব্রতা যথাসম্ভব দূর করে পরিবেষণ করতে হয়েচে পদ্যানুবাদে ।

লেখকের অনূদিত মেঘদূতটির মত ঋতুসংহারের পদ্যানুবাদকালে মূল কাব্যের ভাব ও শব্দঝঙ্কার বাঙলা ভাষায় যতটা ফোটানো যেতে পারে তারই চেষ্টা করা হয়েচে—মূল সংস্কৃত ছন্দের হুবহু অনুকরণ না ক'রে । তাই পংক্তি গণনায় অনুবাদে ভাব ও ছন্দ-ঝঙ্কার বজায় রাখতে গিয়ে কাথাওবা কাথাও বশী পদ হয়ে গেছে । কৃত্রিমভাবে শব্দসংকোচন দ্বারা পদপূরণের পন্থা খোঁজা হয়নি । যে যে স্থানে পদপূরণের জন্য মূল কাব্যটিকে ছাড়িয়ে গেছে, সে সব যায়গায় *** এইরূপ চিহ্ন দিয়ে দেখানো হয়েচে । অবশ্য এক্ষেত্রেও যতটা পারা গেছে মূল শ্লোকটির ভাবার্থ অবলম্বন ক'রে তার অনুরূপ ভাব ব্যঞ্জক কথার দ্বারা পদপূরণ করা হয়েচে । এই 'খোদার উপর খোদকারী' মহাকবি কালিদাসের মূল কাব্যের রস পরিবেষণের খাতিরে করতে হয়েচে ব'লে আশাকরি গুণী সমাজের নিকট ক্ষমার্হ হ'ব ।

মৎরচিত মেঘদূতের পদ্যানুবাদ দেখে প্রীত হ'য়ে স্বর্গীয় বন্ধু ডক্টর নরেন্দ্রনাথ সেনগুপ্ত মহাশয় ঋতুসংহারটিরও অনুবাদ করতে উৎসাহিত করেন । বড়ই দুঃখর বিষয় তিনি আর ইহজগতে নাই,- তাই তাঁর স্মৃতিতর্পণের জন্য তাঁরই নামে কাব্যটি উৎসর্গ করা গেল । সচিত্র পাণ্ডুলিপি প্রণয়নের আনুপ্রেরণা দেন 'দি ইণ্ডিয়ান প্রেস লিমিটেড'র অধ্যক্ষ বন্ধুবর হরিকেশব ঘোষ মহাশয় এবং তিনিই প্রকাশের সুব্যবস্থা করে দেওয়ায় চিরঋণ আবদ্ধ করেচেন ।

মহাকবির এই কাব্যের যোগ্য পদ্যানুবাদ করার ক্ষমতা না থাকলেও রস গ্রহণের যেটুকু শক্তি আছে তারই উপর নির্ভর করে রস পরিবেষণের অসাধ্য সাধন করেত গেছি—এখন ফলাফল গুণীজন সমাজের হাতে দিয়ে নিশ্চিন্ত রইলাম । মহাকবির কাব্যের চিত্রগুলি আঁকার লোভ বহুকাল থেকে ছিল ; তার সুযোগ এতকাল পরে হল এইসূত্রে ।

পরিশেষ বলা প্রয়োজন যে ঋতুসংহারের পদ্যানুবাদটির ছন্দ ধরতে গেলে প্রত্যেক লাইনের প্রথম অক্ষর এবং সপ্তম অক্ষর ছন্দ ও যতি বুঝে জোর দিয়ে পড়তে হবে যথা—

নিদাঘের কাল । সমাগত প্রিয়া

ভাস্কর কর । প্রচণ্ড অতি । শ্রীঅসিতকুমার হালদার
লক্ষ্ণৌ, বাদশাবাগ ।
২৬শে ভাদ্র ১৩৫১

Editor's Introduction
Debashish Banerji

A conventional way of understanding this book is as a trilingual presentation of Kalidasa's Ṛtusaṃhāra; or rather, a bilingual translation of Kalidasa's Sanskrit poem on the pageant of the six Indian seasons. As Richard Hartz points out in his essay on the Seasons, the value of such an undertaking would be the furtherance of the genre of "world literature," announced by Goethe in the early 19th c., in a context related to the early modern transmission of Kalidasa to Germany. In this announcement Goethe recognized the arrival of a global world, so much more realized in our times. This contemporary realization, however, is not one of shared world cultures on an equal footing. Mediated by the history of colonialism and contemporary capitalism, cultures exist along a power gradient of contested normativity and significance. At one time, as Hartz notes, the Sanskrit cosmopolis that formed the readership of Kalidasa, had extended reach; today, even among Indians, few feel the need to learn Sanskrit, except for a minority with a specialized interest in its literatures or as part of an emerging nationalism rooted in Sanskrit seen as "pure origin." There are many more Bengali readers than readers of Sanskrit, whose curiosity in Indian cultural history may be somewhat assuaged reading a Bengali translation. But in our contemporary postcolonial and global condition of diasporic dispersions and corporate overdetermination, increasing numbers of Bengali speakers are unable to read their mother-tongue and are versed only in English. For such readers, an English translation may be their only access to the classical tradition of Sanskrit literature as well as to the literature of their mother-tongue.

What Goethe had in mind when he spoke about a "world literature," is perhaps a horizon of new world subjectivity, arising from exposure to and engagement with world cultures. As a creative writer of genius the contact with a vast corpus of alien cultural expression undoubtedly afforded him an enlargement of imagination and expressive power. About a century after Goethe, and as part of a cultural context shared by Asit Haldar, author of our Bengali translation, the Bengali poet and litterateur Rabindranath Tagore reiterated the modern necessity of world literature for enabling a transcendence of insular cultural values or doxa and enlargement of consciousness through engagement with cultural alterity. Tagore saw such subjective world cultural engagements as conceptual journeys that would activate "arguments with and doubts about" (*yukti tarka o sandeher udbhav*) the biases and hidden assumptions of one's own culture, leading to enrichment for "all voyagers on the path of progress" (*unnatipather jātri*) from different locations and times.[1]

This positive potential towards what one might call "integral culture," not decided by a predetermined or foreclosed canon but arising from expanding individual cultural engagements is not absent from our times. It requires a literate creative synthetic sensibility that sociologists Paul Ray and Sherry Ruth Anderson have identified as a trait in a section of educated contemporary world population they have called "cultural creatives" in an eponymous book published in 2000. Perhaps a trilingual text is best suited for audiences of this kind. Though the authors of *Cultural Creatives: How 50 Million People are Changing the World* are optimistic about the revolutionary potential of this population to steer the world towards an "integral culture," it is important not to ignore the more obvious neo-liberal global culture growing up around us. This kind of world culture identifies, commodifies and packages all ethnic expressions for passive surface consumption as varieties or flavors of exotic entertainment. Considering the subject matter of Kalidasa's seasons, for example, as vivid aesthetic idealizations of flora and fauna and sensuous or erotically inflected femininity expressed in different seasons, literal

---

[1] Tagore, "Samudra Jatra" as quoted in De, Esha Niyogi. "Decolonizing Universality: Postcolonial Theory and the Quandary of Ethical Agency", pg. 1.

instances of such content leaving nothing to the imagination are streamed continuously and repeatedly in sensationally gratifying variations through a variety of television channels or are readily available as "standing reserve" at the press of a button through innumerable websites. Given this severely compromised and limited readership, what value may we find in a trilingual presentation of a 5th c. Sanskrit poem?

To answer this question adequately, I feel we should look a little more carefully at our three texts, considering them in their historical and spatial contexts. Seen this way, it is not a single text translated into two other languages but rebirths expressing unique and very different cultural temporalities and spatialities that confront us in our voyage of the mind towards self-enlargement. We see how the fertility of a text like *Ṛtusaṃhāra* occasions its repeated returns under different conditions serving new audiences with different needs and expectations; and how each return in a new cultural context has a power to affect its historicity and spatiality in unique ways. This engagement with the pluripotency of a text that has traveled through world history and is accessible and active in our global space and time is a powerful aid to universalization as well as to civilization studies.

I

To dwell for a moment on the origin of this poem – as Hartz mentions in his Introduction, not much is known about the poet except that he probably lived in the 5th c. as a court poet of the Gupta emperor Chandragupta II (r. c. 375-410 CE) and is adulated for his vivid metaphoricity and near-synesthetic turn of expression. He is considered one of the architects of a classicism in Sanskrit literature that became canonical and influenced much of Sanskrit poetry that came after and later, vernacular Indian poetry. This classicism in literature was itself part of a larger revolution inaugurating an age of integrated classical culture including art, music, architecture and elite urban (*nāgarika*) conduct throughout India. Hartz has referred to this in terms of Sheldon Pollock's conception of the formation of a Sanskrit cosmopolis.² This self-consciousness of new creation is powerfully present in Kalidasa's texts.

His patron Chandragupta Vikramaditya, along with his predecessors Chandragupta I (r. c. 319-335 ce) and Samudragupta (r. 335-375 ce) had extended for themselves an empire that spread from sea to sea across North India and exerted hegemonic political and cultural influence over much of the rest of India. More ideologically, the Guptas put an end to several centuries of rulership over North India by Central Asian and West Asian kings. Chandragupta II carefully fashioned his dynastic identity as a savior of Bharatvarsha from "foreigners," taking as one of his titles Shākāri or enemy of the Śākas (Scythians/Central Asians). Part of the promotion of his self-image was achieved through propagandist culture, as may be seen in the spectacular Varaha panel at Udaygiri in Madhya Pradesh.³ Intimately related to this was the textualization of a synthetic Hindu theology, narrativized in the Puranas and Tantras and canonically inherited by all Hindus thereafter. The powerfully nationalistic age he inaugurated was territorialized through the establishment of a cultural imaginary saturated with affect. For example, some scholars have suggested that Kalidasa's *Meghadūtam*, which is a more mature work than *Ṛtusaṃhāra*, can be read as a nostalgic recounting of a beloved geography by the poet, despatched temporarily from Chandragupta's court in Ujjain to accompany his daughter Prabhavati as dowry for her marriage with the Vakataka prince of the Deccan. However possible this circumstance, it is at least as likely an example of cultural territorialization through imaginative appropriation. The association of an imperial geography with elite cultural tropes of affect and eros generated in the imperial court and disseminated by the medium of literature or art produces and normalizes complexes of sense-perception and feeling through the literary and/or

---

2 Sheldon Pollock, *The Language of the Gods*.
3 The earliest example of monumental Hindu art, it portrays a number of visual puns establishing Chandragupta II as the savior of India. See Michael Willis, *The Archeology of Hindu Ritual*, pp. 41-64.

visual sphere of influence. Producing taste and emotion such memes become canonical through distribution, repetition and teaching and exert agency on those partaking of the culture through the centuries, until supplanted by new powerful tropes of greater relevance to a new time and space; and even then, they remain potentia for creative reuse.

The *Ṛtusaṃhāra* may also be seen as an instance in this process. Hartz has drawn attention to the close similarity in expressive tropes between Kalidasa's seasons and the roughly contemporaneous *Midnight Songs* of China. Such similarity, he notes, is presently thought to be coincidental, but the quatrain form of the Sanskrit poem is thought by scholars like Victor Mair and Tsu-Lin Mei to have been adapted by Recent Style Tang poetry in the 6th c.[4] Mair also discusses the adaptation of the "Six Limbs of Indian Painting" (Ṣaḍaṅga) thought to originate around the same period (c. 4th – 5th c.) in Xie He's Six Canons of Chinese Painting written in the early 6th c., demonstrating the continental spread of Gupta cultural memes.[5] Moreover, the seasons may be considered the temporal counterpart of regional specificity (as in the Meghadūta), and an opportunity to establish a mnemonic of annual changes marking territory and culture. We see a signal example of this in the case of Japan from the 10th-12th centuries. In the late 9th c., the Heian court restricted contact with China leading to an inward turn and the development of a nationalistic Japanese culture. The cultural expressions of this period distinguished themselves from Chinese models in both style and content. Content-wise a celebration of specific geographic locations and seasonal activities formed the core of this move towards identity. Genres of *waka* poetry and *Yamato-e* painting established themselves, with *shiki-e* or seasonal paintings as an oft-repeated sub-genre.[6] These creative genres

---

4 Mair, Victor H. and Mei, Tsu-Lin, "The Sanskrit Origins of Recent Style Prosody."
5 Mair, Victor H. "Xie He's 'Six Laws' of Painting and Their Indian Parallels," in Zong-qi Cai, ed., *Chinese Aesthetics..*, p. 97.
6 See Leisinger, Andreas. "Exhibition Review: Yamato-e, Japanese Painting…, pp. 69–73.

also led to self-conscious seasonal activities, such as gatherings to view cherry blossoms in Spring or the full moon in Autumn. From the 13th c., Japan witnessed several alterations of predominantly Sinophilic and Sinophobic phases, but through all these both literary and artistic seasonal genres remained popular.

Hartz also draws attention to the specifically Indian precedents to Kalidasa's depiction of the seasons – the Vedic notion of order, *ṛtam*, structuring the changes of the world and the Upanishadic goal of bliss, *ānanda*, experienceable through impersonal affect, *rasa*, in all the expressions of the world. Indeed this backdrop cannot be neglected and needs to be related to the way in which Gupta classical culture represents an attempt to spiritualize elite secular life-experience. The Viṣṇudharmottara Purāṇa, also codified around the 5th c., includes a section called the Citrasūtra, that canonizes some of the associations of the seasons for painting. Whether these conventions originate in the Ṛtusaṃhāra is difficult to ascertain but it is certainly likely. Following such canons, the covert function of inspiring a union (yoga) of sensuous affect and spiritual experience through seasonal expression continued to animate Indian poetry through the centuries in Sanskrit and vernacular languages and in painting from the 16th – 19th c., in a variety of regions. A popular later approach to the seasons was the Bārahmāsā or twelve month cycle, that continued the Ṛtusaṃhāra's convention of vivid descriptions of changing nature during the twelve months, related to amorous and erotic moods between lovers (nāyaka and nāyikā).[7] A particularly popular post-16th c. text dealing with the Bārahmāsā was Keshavadas' Rasikapriyā, which also became a favorite with artists of the Pahari (hill) states of North India. As part of the post-16th c. popularization of Krishna bhakti (devotion), many depictions of the Rasikapriya featured Krishna as the lover and Radha as his beloved, highlighting the pageant of seasons as

---

7   See Deshmukh, S. B. *Baramasa Paintings*.

spiritual moods of the Divine in relation to the human soul.[8]

II

If this provides us some context to the Ṛtusaṃhāra in its origin as a text embodying affects that propagated and repeated variously in the pre-modern world, Asit Kuman Haldar's Bengali translation of this text brings us into the modern period. Haldar (1890-1964) was born in Jorasanko, Calcutta (now Kolkata) in 1890. Jorasanko was the extended family home of a branch of the Tagores (Bengali: Thakur), who were a prominent educated family of 19th and early 20th c. Calcutta, well known for their cultural activities. A number of creative personalities of public renown came from this extended community, the most famous of whom was Rabindranath Tagore (1861-1941), already mentioned, a poet who was the first non-Western person to be awarded the Nobel Prize for Literature in 1913, an event that needs to be viewed in the context of our discussion of modernity and "world literature." A nephew of Rabindranath, Abanindranath Tagore (1871-1951), also from Jorasanko, was an artist of national and international stature, and founder of a school of "national painting," now known as the Bengal School of Art. Haldar was a grand-nephew of Rabindranath and a nephew of Abanindranath. He became an art student at the Calcutta Govt. Art College in 1904 and studied under Abanindranath, forming part of the first generation of Bengal School artists.

Calcutta had been the capital of the mercantile operations of the British East India Company since 1772. As an aid to the trading operations of the British, a class of middlemen had emerged in Calcutta, who had versed themselves in the language and conventions of the British and constituted an educated gentry (*bhadralok*) that mediated the worlds of tradition and modernity. It has been noted that the cultural response of the bhadralok to colonial presence in Calcutta was split between revival and reform, but

---

[8] Harsha Dehejia's *Rasikapriya: Ritikavya of Keshavadas* includes a translation of the poem in English and 470 paintings based on the poem.

though these oppositional categories had some social currency in turn of the 19th/20th c. Calcutta, it would be more correct to say that a complex braiding of conservative and liberal attitudes developed and co-existed to constitute a critical and creative response to colonialism, modernity and an emergent regionalism and nationalism. Whereas natives experienced instrumentalization, exploitation and oppression from the British, the opening up of a hybrid urban space brought to question the biases and internal hierarchies of native society and made possible the creative exploitation of blurred cultural conventions. It also brought the values of the Enlightenment, such as the equality of all humans, based on rationality, universal education, social upliftment and liberation of women. Outcaste Brahmins from East Bengal, the Tagores were beneficiaries of the opportunities available due to the cultural uncertainty of the modern polis and the freedom of both sexes to pursue lifestyles of their choice. At the same time, they became acutely conscious of the erosion of native cultural forms due to civilizational devaluation and joined others of their place and time to participate in a movement of cultural nationalism which has been called the Bengal Renaissance.[9] Through various forms of culture, such as poetry, fiction, essays, theater, song and art, several members from among the Jorasanko Tagores joined other like-minded native citizens in critiquing colonialism and modernity and re-engaging with traditional cultural forms, disseminating their expressions among Calcutta bhadralok through public events, print journalism, entertainment and formal and informal forums of learning and exchange.

Colonialism itself is a fractured discourse, made up on one side of mercantile and political exploitation, on another of an effort at spreading and normalizing the rational values of the Enlightenment, its "white man's burden," and in a third direction, of promoting native culture as part of an internal Romantic critique of Enlightenment ideals and values.

---

9 For a good contemporary introduction to the Bengal Renaissance, read Subrata Dasgupta's *Awakening: The Story of the Bengal Renaissance*.

It is this third direction that was shorn of its pretensions of benefaction in the book *Orientalism* by Edward W. Said published in 1978. Said's take-down revealed Orientalism to be a device for Western stereotyping of the Orient, subjecting it to a static essentialism that rendered it a living museum of the West, denied agency and made fit for exotic consumption. Many scholars have extended Said to talk of nationalism as an inverse Orientalism, an essentialist nativism.[10] There is undoubtedly some truth to this view,[11] but 40+ years since Said's persuasive rhetoric, this understanding of Orientalism has been nuanced to make visible a strand of transcultural dialogic critique of modernity by affective communities interested in alternative trajectories of modernity.[12] It is not that the participants of such communities held to homogeneous views, but their alliances overlapped and found strategic common ground to launch the material foundations of their visions. One such transnational community developed around the Govt. College of Arts and Crafts in Calcutta at the start of the 20th c. involving Abanindranath Tagore and his students.

The Orientalist background to this nexus must be sought in the anti-utilitarian critique of the Arts and Crafts movement in Britain. Taking advantage of the Great Exhibition of London of 1851, in which crafts of Britain's colonies were displayed, members of the Arts and Crafts circle initiated strident debates on the decline of artistic quality in British manufacture, calling for partnerships with the living traditions of colonial arts so as to further their skills while at the same time drawing on these to revitalize British industrial design. This led to the founding

---

10 See, for example Partha Chatterjee, *The Nation and its Fragments*, Chapter One, "Whose Imagined Community," pp. 3-13. In the context of art in Indian nationalism, see Partha Mitter, *Art and Nationalism in Colonial India*, 7, and Tapati Guha-Thakurta, *The Making of a New Indian Art*, as discussed in Banerji, *Alternate Nation*, xxi-xxii.

11 Inverse or reverse Orientalism has in fact been a powerful contributing factor to the rise of right-wing politics in contemporary India. See Thomas Blum Hansen, *The Saffron Wave*.

12 See Leela Gandhi, *Affective Communities*.

of the Victoria and Albert Museum and art school in London, followed by a number of colleges of arts and crafts in India, among the earliest being that of Calcutta in 1854.[13] These colleges were dominated by teachers from the Arts and Crafts circle. One of these teachers, Ernest Binfield Havell, came to Calcutta as the Superintendent of its Art College in 1896. Havell took steps to teach traditional arts and crafts at the art school, replacing European models and methods by Indian ones. Havell also wrote extensively on Indian Art and may be considered among the founders of Indian art history.[14] In his view the Indian art canon was centered in the classical culture of the Gupta period, of which, as we have seen, Kalidasa was a prime literary representative. Havell formed a partnership with Abanindranath Tagore establishing him as the Vice Principal of the College in 1905.[15] Asit Haldar joined the school in 1906 among the first batch of Abanindranath's students.

Though Abanindranath and his early students set about re-engaging with Indian artistic and literary traditions, Abanindranath, unlike Havell, was not invested in promoting a privileged art historical Indian canon. Apart from an engagement with national traditions, as a subject who found himself in the community of the Bengal Renaissance, he was also interested in a Bengali regionalism. Moreover, in 1902, Abanindranath encountered Okakura Kakuzo, a Japanese ideologue and inspirer of a nationalistic art movement, Nihonga, from whom he imbibed a vision and inspiration for a pan-Asian identity as a consolidated continental response to Western civilizational hegemony.[16] Finally, it needs to be realized that what colonialism brought to India was a larger epistemic transformation which originated in Europe but was imposed on India. This transformation, which marked the modern from the premodern, was accompanied by cultural evaluation and critique in the regions of

---

13 See Debashish Banerji *The Alternate Nation of Abanindranath Tagore*, 25-27.
14 Ibid.
15 Ibid.
16 See Banerji, *Alternate Nation*, xl, 38-42.

its origin as part of its normalization. In the reaction to its establishment in India, Abanindranath felt the need for independent engagement, evaluation and critique in the act of painting. Thus, what he practiced and promoted among his students was an individual engagement with the traditions of the past vis-à-vis the forces of colonialism and modernity. This engagement enacted the artist's sense of belonging to the variety of emergent forms of identity resulting from the encounter of colonialism and nationalism with its internal vectors of positivism, romanticism, pan-Asianism, regionalism and nationalism.[17]

1905, the year of inception of the Bengal School, was a landmark year in the history of the Bengal Renaissance, because what had been preparing culturally for a century erupted into the anticolonial political agitation known as the swadeshi movement from that year. The cultural politics of the Bengal Renaissance continued now as part of the overt struggle for national independence that had been born irreversibly. Abanindranath and his students were swept into this movement. Abanindranath painted an image of Mother India (Bhārat Mātā) which was used in a political rally and other students, such as Nandalal Bose, painted stirring images of goddesses like Kali, exhorting the nation to activism and sacrifice. An assimilation and interpretation of history accompanied this phase. In 1909, at the instance of Sister Nivedita, an Irish disciple of Vivekananda, Abanindranath sent a few of his students, among whom was Asit Haldar, to Ajanta to accompany Lady Christiana Herringham in documenting the 5th c. Buddhist murals in these caves. Considered canonical masterpieces of the Gupta classical period, intimate exposure and the opportunity to copy these paintings was supposed by Indophiles like Havell and Sister Nivedita to facilitate the revival of a classical Indian painting in the modern period.

Abanindranath himself, however, did not go to Ajanta, thereby registering his difference from this over-privileging of a period and a

---

17 Op. cit, xli.

style. But this did not mean he did not support its assimilation as part of a larger sense of belonging. Himself well versed in Sanskrit literature, the moods and ideas of classical aesthetics formed an essential part of his lifelong engagement. His paintings of this early period include a number of themes directly derived from Kalidasa or tropes pervading the classical canon of his period, such as Yaksha's Lament (Meghadūta) and Abhisarika. He wrote two short monographs on classical aesthetics, one a discussion of the Six Limbs of Indian Painting (Ṣaḍanga) (discussed above) and another on the metaphoricity of classical Indian anatomy. Straddling the worlds of art and literature, his literary expression began with a retelling of Kalidasa's Shakuntala. Yet such an engagement with Indian classicism co-existed within a comparative framework of world culture, whose instances spanned Europe and Japan, Mughal paintings, Bengali rural arts and urban street culture; and he encouraged his students too to fashion their responses to colonialism and modernity from an assimilation and synthesis of varied homologous sources of creativity and critique. One can see in this eclectic and quintessentially modern engagement and embodying of the tenet of world culture referred to earlier in the words of Rabindranath Tagore.

The Bengal School's response to colonialism and modernity occurred within a dialogic frame with Orientalism.[18] Bengal School artists often selected Orientalist favorites to attain visibility, but depicted these in a fashion that expressed regional, national and pan-Asian nuances and tropes, often ambiguous or untranslatable in prevailing Orientalist convention and hence inviting dialog and transformation of perception and understanding. Following Abanindranath, Asit Kumar Haldar selected a number of such Orientalist Asian and Indian themes for depiction. These included the Life of Buddha, the Rubaiyat of Omar Khayyam and a series on the History of India. Among Abanindranath's students, Asit Haldar was the only one who, like his teacher, also expressed himself in

---

18 See the discussion of hybridity in Banerji, *Alternate Nation*, xxix-xli.

the literary arts. This endeared him to Rabindranath, himself a poet who appreciated painting, turning his hand to it in his late years.

In 1911, Rabindranath invited Haldar to teach art at his experimental center of learning, Viśva-Bhārati in Shantiniketan. The choice of the name Viśva Bhārati for his educational institution, speaks of Tagore's view of nationalism. The phrase is a collocation of "universe" or "world" and "India," indicating a nexus facilitating the porous engagement of national history and world history. It also denotes an integration of earth and world, nature as represented by the local/regional geosphere and biosphere and the national and global world of culture in a symbolic communitarian space. Haldar spent the major part of over a decade in Shantiniketan, teaching and establishing the art school, known to this day as Kalā Bhavana (Art House) between 1919 and 1921. Here he was joined by two other early students of Abanindranath, Surendranath Kar (joined 1917) and Nandalal Bose (joined 1919), working with them to establish some of the extended ideas of the Bengal School in an alternative social environment.[19] The continuation and furtherance of the British Arts and Crafts movement in these ideas, as transmitted through the relationship of Havell and Abanindranath at the Govt. Art College, should not be lost sight of. Under the encouragement and inspiration of Rabindranath, Haldar and his companions worked to make art an integral aspect of the social habitus of Shantiniketan, through book illustration, architecture, furniture design, sculpture, murals, festivals, theater, temporary decoration and ritual,[20] all expressing ideas central to the world historical telos of an integrated global village aimed for by Viśva-Bhārati and expressed in its motto, "Where the world becomes a single nest" (*yatra viśvam bhavati ekanīḍam*). As mentioned, the integral social habitus of Shantiniketan, as Rabindranath conceived it, included a relationship of cultures with the situated life of nature. The intimacy to the earth and its changes was

---

19 A brief biographical sketch of Asit Haldar may be found at the Visva-Bharati website: http://www.visvabharati.ac.in/AsitkumarHaldar.html (last accessed 7/24/2021).
20 Ibid.

emphasized through seasonal events constituted by fairs, theater, songs and a visual rituality of temporal earth practices. Shantiniketan came alive collectively during the monsoons with barsha-mongol, in autumn with sharodotsab, in winter with poush-mela and in spring with basanta utsab. Ploughing and tree planting ceremonies (halakarshan and brikkharopon) as well as a celebration of the Bengali New Year (poila boisakh) along with the poet's birthday (panchise boisakh) made up the annual seasonal calendar. These intentions behind the honoring of the earth and the reclamation of space owned by the alienated commodities of modernity through the expression of human culture in embodied objects of singular creative consciousness such as illustrated and hand-printed books highlighting visuality, literacy and seasonal context, should be kept in mind when thinking about Asit Haldar's translation of the Ṛtusaṃhāra as a rebirth of the text in the space-time of modern India and Bengal.

As if through a series of transplantations involving progressively enlarging nurseries leading to the open spaces of the world, Haldar traveled in Europe for a year in 1923 and returned to join, at first, the Jaipur College of Arts and Crafts and then the Lucknow Govt Art College as its principal in 1925. Till his retirement in 1955, Haldar produced the major portion of his paintings and writings here. The Ṛtusamhāra translation and paintings were done here in 1941. Around the extended efforts of the Bengal School to create a household visual culture manifesting a depth dimension, a variety of collaborative services developed. Among these was the print shop, Indian Press founded by Chintamoni Ghosh in Allahabad. From 1908 to 1922, Indian Press published all the works of Rabindranath Tagore.[21] Chintamoni Ghosh's son, Hari Keshav Ghosh continued his father's business and undertook to publish Asit Haldar's

---

21 See the article by Arindam Ghosh, present Director of Indian Press in the electronic magazine Different Truths. Nov. 4, 2017: https://www.differenttruths.com/travel-getaways/history-culture/people/tagore-and-allahabad-indian-press-published-all-his-books-from-1908-14-including-the-nobel-prize-winning-gitanjali-i/ (last accessed 7/24/2021).

books. In the Bengali Introduction to his translation Haldar acknowledges the encouragement of Hari Keshav Ghosh for publishing the translation accompanied by his paintings of the seasons. Haldar also acknowledges Dr. Narendranath Sengupta, who had read Haldar's earlier translation of Kalidasa's Meghadūta and felt inspired to encourage him to translate the Ṛtusamhāra. He had passed away before the publication of the translation and Haldar regrets this fact and dedicates his book to him.

Haldar's translation is printed in his calligraphic hand on hand-made paper with seven inserted color plates and line drawings on each page. While each section featuring a season starts with a corresponding painting, the first color plate features a composite of all the seasons personified as females bearing a symbolic representative gift and winding up a path which ends in the floral beatitude of Spring. Preceding Spring, the season of Dew (śiśira) is a ghostly shade swaddled in vaporous garb. The specific illustrations of the seasons merit some consideration in relation to the text. The first features a bathing woman and is clearly taken from the first stanza of the poem. The second, depicting the monsoon, shows dark overhanging storm clouds above a terrace where a woman, her upper garment flying behind her, her left arm raised as if to shelter from the storm, rushes indoors, while a peacock on a column, watches her with lowered head. There is no single verse which fits this illustration, which may be thought a composite imagination of the artist, extrapolating perhaps from verses 21 and 22. The image for autumn combining fleecy white clouds, paddy fields, white kasha rushes and large red-headed storks seems a loose rendering of verse 1. For winter, we see a nāyikā with a wistful look holding what seems like a bowl in one hand and touching her lower lip with the other. This is clearly a depiction of verse 13 where at break of day a young woman watches herself in a mirror while applying cosmetics to her face and feeling the bite marks of her lover on her lower lip. Similarly, the image for the dewy season seems to be loosely adapted from a single verse, verse 5, which speaks of a nāyikā with betel-rolls, cosmetics and garlands, entering her bedchamber redolent with agarwood incense smoke. In the painting, the lady has an incense burner with smoke emanating, walking into a room. The image for Spring shows lovers seated in a relaxed intimate posture against bolsters, an incense burner at their feet. There is no single verse that describes such a scene but the entire canto being full of descriptions of amorous nāyikās, this can also be thought of as a creative depiction of the general mood. The line drawings on each page amplify the referents of each season. What is interesting here is the regionalism of these drawings, carrying the flavor of Haldar's many years in the rural environs of Shantiniketan observing the life of nature. In comparing the illustrations with the text, one feature which draws the attention is that the text has many overt descriptions of female erotic sensuousness but these features are downplayed in the illustrations. Even when scenes of such passages are illustrated, as with the nāyikā of winter, they are modulated to a subtler mood. One may see in the artwork here the long tradition of bārahmāsā paintings, where the seasons become representations of the affective moods of love. It is as if Haldar's perception of Kalidasa's seasons is one of the female soul, Anima in Jungian terminology, passing through moods of affect towards the Divine Male. This kind of view is endemic to Vaishnavism and exemplified in the bārahmāsā paintings of the Himalayan hill states (Pahāri).

To summarize, in considering Asit Haldar's translation as a rebirth of the Ṛtusamhāra related to our times and to the space of an emerging nationalism, regionalism and pan-Asianism, we should see it as an epistemic response, a response of cultural politics and a social response. As an epistemic response, it is a reinvocation of the circular time of premodernity vis-à-vis the fleeting instrumentalized clock-time of modernity. The stability of the seasons with their geological, zoological and cultural invariants return us to a sense of the large cycles of nature and life helping to provide an archetypal connection in the midst of the "lost time" of modernity. This leads to the cultural response. As a trope familiar to Orientalists, the seasons and particularly, Kalidasa's poem, opens a space for regional, national and pan-Asian imagery. As in the case of Abanindranath's illustrations of Orientalist favorites, Asit Haldar's illustrations and line drawings highlighted a regional interpretation of the descriptions. Haldar was also familiar with the traditions of Bārahmāsā paintings as well as of the East Asian, particularly Japanese season paintings, which he studied from the issues of the magazine Kokka, sent by Okakura, whom he met in 2011. The influence of these larger traditions also subtly weave themselves into his translations and paintings, giving an amplified and porous scope to modern Bengali regionalism and a regional specificity to nationalism and Orientalism, as per the vision of Rabindranath's Viśva Bhārati. The poetics of classical sensuous spirituality mentioned by Hartz also features in this cultural response, introducing a transformative vision into the everyday lives of modern Indian subjects and a sense of historical depth to their colonized lives.[22] Finally, in terms of a social response, the handwritten, illustrated and finely produced book propagates a vision of a social space of human depth to modify a mechanized surface utilitarianism of modern life.

III

Coming now to the third and final "rebirth" of the text in the English translation by Richard Hartz, this contemporary version brings the book fully into the era of global history and world literature. I use these terms in the ambiguous sense introduced at the start of this introduction. A culturally fragmented and diasporic condition occupies the world today,

---

[22] Rabindranath Tagore's poem Banshi (Flute) from his collection of poems *Punascha* of 1932 provides a vivid example of the dignity and spiritual height of Indian classical music transforming the life of an utterly impoverished clerk of Calcutta. A neighbor occasionally plays the Indian classical raga sindhu-bhairav on the shehnai lifting the wretched conditions towards the heavens of eternity. A translation by Kumud Biswas titled Kinu Goala's Alley may be found at https://allpoetry.com/Kinu-Goalas-Alley--English-Translation (last accessed 7/24/2021).

at the service of neo-liberal globalization. To this world, Kalidasa is a name in General Knowledge textbooks and translations of his books exist in glossy coffee table paperbacks as a form of cultural capital for the consumption of status conscious business executives. At the same time, alternative enclaves of world citizenship like Shantiniketan, have developed in a variety of locations, in which the Ṛtusamhāra and its translations may be seen as serving the kind of convergent purpose of integral culture dreamed of by Rabindranath. One such location is the Sri Aurobindo Ashram in Pondicherry, South India founded by Indian spiritual teacher and philosopher, Sri Aurobindo (1872-1950). Sri Aurobindo was one of the founders of the struggle for Indian independence referred to in the section on Asit Haldar and a theorist and ideologue for the swadeshi movement which started in Calcutta in 1905. He was also well versed in the classical tradition of Indian literature, as Hartz's essay indicates through several quotes on Kalidasa by him. He gave the name integral yoga to the form of spiritual praxis that he developed and taught in his yoga ashram at Pondicherry. The term "integral" in integral yoga encompasses three kinds of integration in response to the fragmented nature of human existence.[23] Firstly, psychological integration, based on the premise that human beings are made up of disparate psychological modes of consciousness and a variety of personalities embodying these modes. Secondly, cosmic or spiritual integration, based on the premise that soul and Nature are divided in our experience as are the varieties of cosmic ideologies and cultural and national histories that constitute global humanity. Thirdly, what he called supramental integration based on the aspiration to overcome the ontological division of the One and the Many as well as Spirit and Matter. Though fundamentally a form

---

23 See Sri Aurobindo, "The Triple Transformation" in *The Life Divine*, 922-952. Also, Bahman Shirazi, following Haridas Cahudhuri has called these three kinds of integration egocentric, psychocentric and cosmocentric. See Shirazi, "Haridas Chaudhuri's Contributions to Integral Psychology" in Debashish Banerji ed., *Integral Yoga Psychology*, 143-158.

of psychological praxis leading to transformation of self and nature, the cultural dimension was included in the praxis. Sri Aurobindo's primary text on yoga, The *Synthesis of Yoga*, starts with an epigram, "All Life is Yoga," making all life activities as channels of spiritual praxis. Literary engagement through writing and/or reading, can be an important means to this end.

Educated in the Classics in England, well-read in modern European languages such as French, Italian, Spanish and German and knowledgeable in Sanskrit, Bengali, Marathi, Gujarati, Hindi and some Tamil among Indian languages,[24] Sri Aurobindo possessed the ideal sensibility for world literature understood as a modern global consciousness or "integral culture." In his words, "Language is the sign of the cultural life of a people, the index of its soul in thought and mind that stands behind and enriches its soul in action."[25] Students at the ashram school learn at least three languages, English, French and Sanskrit, apart from their Indian mother-tongue learned at home. As a result of Sri Aurobindo's and his spiritual collaborator, the Mother's encouragement of language learning, several students know upward of five languages by the time they leave school. Particularly, while Sri Aurobindo and the Mother were alive, their ashram attracted disciples from across India and from several countries of the world to form a cosmopolitan space of world culture.

In his social and political writings, particularly the texts The Human Cycle and The Ideal of Human Unity, Sri Aurobindo developed a philosophy of history according to which, from a world historical viewpoint, humanity had passed through an Age of Convention during the European medieval "Dark Ages," reacted to this in an Age of Individualism in the Cycle of Reason starting from the European Renaissance and Enlightenment and was in the transition to an Age of Subjectivism in 20th c. modernity.[26] Subjectivism may exacerbate

---

24 Peter Heehs, *The Lives of Sri Aurobindo*, 43.
25 Sri Aurobindo, "Diversity in Oneness" in The Ideal of Human Unity, 519.
26 Sri Aurobindo, The Human Cycle, 13-14.

difference; it tries to contain this through the search for rational laws governing all things, but below this the hidden drives of nature push towards expression. Modern psychology is largely a discovery of this hidden bulk of the iceberg of human consciousness. At the national level, subjectivism consolidates itself into a mythic cultural history which unites a people subjectively. Sri Aurobindo considers both the case of individual subjectivism as in the creative cultural expressions of Modernism,[27] and national subjectivism as expressed in ethnic and national mythologies.[28] The discussion of national subjectivism may be considered a continuation of the thinking with which Sri Aurobindo participated in early Indian nationalism. At the same time, it represents the hindsight of one World War and in its revision, two World Wars. Sri Aurobindo points to the dangers of ethnocentrism and racism, using Germany as an example.[29] He then invokes the soul as the center of true subjectivism. The soul, according to Sri Aurobindo, is unique in each individual and collective, yet it is a unique formation of the same Divine Substance with infinite capacity for variation. At the center of our subjective expressions and relations, the soul enjoys the differences it confronts while intuiting identity behind it.[30] Today the talk of a soul, particularly a nation-soul sounds outmoded if not dangerous, but it is easy to think of common human origins or even ontological origins, which have developed differently over time, forming unique cultural histories. If related to in depth, they may enjoy a deep kinship in what seems radical difference.

Instead of a subjectivism of the soul, what we see more commonly is a subjectivism of "the vital" or life-self, made up of emotions, wants and passions.[31] This is what has made subjectivism a fearful proposition

---

27 Sri Aurobindo, "The Coming of the Subjective Age," The Human Cycle, 30-31.
28 Sri Aurobindo, "The Discovery of the Nation-Soul," The Human Cycle, 35-43.
29 Sri Aurobindo, "True and False Subjectivism," The Human Cycle, 44-54.
30 Ibid.
31 Sri Aurobindo, "Civilization and Barbarism," The Human Cycle, 73-81.

from the viewpoint of the Reason. But Reason proceeds to classify and organize a world based on distinct properties that hide both true oneness and unique difference. It creates ideological distinctions where there were none in life-experience and leads to the deep alienation which we experience in our times.[32] Only a seeking in depth for the spiritual soul can lead us into the fulfillment of the modern age of cultural and individual diversity, a fulfillment of psychological and universal integration.[33] Engagement with world literature can be a means in this direction.[34] It is interesting to note that Sri Aurobindo was a poet who brought his vast exposure to world literature to bear on his own poetry and poetic criticism. Thinking of the Ṛtusamhāra, in his epic poem Savitri, he began a canto with a description of the seasons which was undoubtedly inspired by Kalidasa.[35] His description expresses a psychic naturalism in which synaesthetic scenes vividly capture the moods of the earth as expressions of divinity leading to Spring seen as a lover who captures the earth-bride in his embrace. Shorn of specific historical contexts, this passage is itself a contemporary translation of the sense of the genre.

Sri Aurobindo passed away in 1950, but in 1968 the Mother founded an international township named Auroville, in proximity to the ashram, with the aspiration of being a space for the realization of human unity as envisaged by Sri Aurobindo, through the subjective engagement of diverse nationalities.[36] The experiment of Auroville continues. Apart from culture, the residents of Auroville attempt to engage spiritually with the geosphere and the biosphere bringing back an integral sense of the

---

32 Sri Aurobindo, "The Reason as Governor of Life" and "The Office and Limitations of Reason," The Human Cycle, 102-123.
33 Sri Aurobindo, The Human Cycle, Chapters XXI-XXIV, 222-269.
34 Sri Aurobindo, "The Suprarational Beauty," The Human Cycle, 142-145.
35 Sri Aurobindo, Book IV: The Book of Birth and Quest, Canto I: The Birth and Childhood of the Flame, Savitri, 349-352.
36 "Auroville will be a site of material and spiritual researches for a living embodiment of an actual human unity." This is the 4th item of the Charter of Auroville given by the Mother. See https://auroville.org/contents/1 (last accessed 7/24/2021).

human habitus.[37]

Richard Hartz, the translator of the Ṛtusamhāra into English is a resident of the Sri Aurobindo ashram since 1980, working at the ashram archives. He studied philosophy at Yale University and South Asian languages and literature at the University of Washington. He is an independent scholar studying Asian languages and cultures with a particular focus on Sanskrit literature and the writings of Sri Aurobindo. His translation attempts to preserve something of the metrical rhythm of the original Sanskrit in the English language. Haldar's translation is also notable for its sensitivity to the meter of the original. However, where Haldar deviates in the line structure of the stanzas, Hartz maintains a stricter adherence to the quatrain. This makes for a compact economy of idea and image in his verses. Moreover, where Haldar's Bengali, because of its closeness to Sanskrit and its continuity in culture, finds it easier to cleave closer to the precise sense of the original, Hartz's English has a much more difficult task of carrying into contemporary English the sense of a culture distant in time and space. Given this fact, his verses capture admirably the import of the original lines, maintaining a fine balance between the natural specificity of Indian names of flora and fauna and universal or international objects, feelings and ideas that make the verses familiar to contemporary international readers.

For those able to read all three versions – as mentioned earlier, there are many at the Sri Aurobindo ashram with this ability – the differences between the three will stand out. The very first verse makes this clear. Whereas the Bengali writes of stored water (bāri sanchaya) depleted by excessive bathing (sadābagāha kṣhata), illustrating this with a woman bathing from a pitcher of water, the English version writes of splashing pools inviting (bathers) all day. As stated in this introduction, translations are not faithful or unfaithful copies of an original, they are trans-creations, originals in their own right in intimate dependence on the version they

---

37 https://auroville.org/contents/516 (last accessed 7/24/2021).

translate.

Finally, the book is being printed by Prisma Press in Auroville. The attention to nature in its changes through the seasons rings particularly appropriate to our times in the environment of Auroville. More than ever before, human rapaciousness has sundered the relation between civilization and nature. It has been said that we live in a new geological era, the Anthropocene,[38] so named because the human footprint has marked the entire geosphere. This mark is the sign of violence and depletion; as a result, the earth's revolt has brought us to the brink of environmental disaster. Auroville is a town that works to heal this relation locally as part of its collective spirituality. The first step in this healing has to come from a change of consciousness; and a first step in this change is a changed relation with the earth. An intimate relation with the seasons and the moods of the earth brings us much closer in consciousness to an integral culture that honors the earth and its creatures.

WORKS CITED

Bahadur, K.P (trans.). *Rasikapriya of Keshavadas*. New Delhi: Motilal Banarasidas. 1990.

Banerji, Debashish. *The Alternate Nation of Abanindranath Tagore*. New Delhi: Sage. 2010.

Banerji, Debashish ed., *Integral Yoga Psychology: Metaphysics and Transformation as Taught by Sri Aurobindo*. Twin Lakes, Wi: Lotus Press. 2020.

Chatterjee, Partha. *The Nation and its Fragments: Colonial and Postcolonial Histories*. Princeton, NJ: Princeton University Press. 1993

Dasgupta Subrata. *Awakening: The Story of the Bengal Renaissance*. New Delhi: Penguin. 2010.

Dawson, Ashley. *Extinction: A Radical History*. New York and London:

---

[38] In its contemporary sense, Anthropocene is a term for our geological era popularized by atmospheric chemist Paul J. Crutzen. See Ashley Dawson's *Extinction: A Radical History*, 19.

OR Books. 2016.

De, Esha Niyogi. "Decolonizing Universality: Postcolonial Theory and the Quandary of Ethical Agency." *Diacritics* ٣٢, no. ٢:(٢٠٠٢) ٤٢-٥٩.

Dehejia, Harsha. *Rasikapriya: Ritikavya of Keshavdas in Ateliers of Love*. Delhi: D.K. Printworld. 2013.

Deshmukh, S. B. *Baramasa Paintings*. Aurangabad: History Museum, Marathwada University. 1992.

Gandhi, Leela. *Affective Communities: Anticolonial Thought, Fin-de-Siecle Radicalism and the Politics of Friendship*. Durham and London: Duke University Press. 2006.

Guha-Thakurta, Tapati. *The Making of a New Indian Art: Artists, Aesthetics and Nationalism in Bengal, c. 1850-1920*. Cambridge: Cambridge University Press. 1992.

Hansen, Thomas Blum. *The Saffron Wave: Democracy and Hindu Nationalism in Modern India*. New Delhi: Oxford India Paperbacks. 2001.

Heehs, Peter. *The Lives of Sri Aurobindo*. New York: Columbia University Press. 2008.

Leisinger, Andreas. "Exhibition Review: Yamato-e, Japanese Painting in the Tradition of Courtly Elegance, Tokyo National Museum." Orientations (May 1994).

Mair, Victor H. and Mei, Tsu-Lin, "The Sanskrit Origins of Recent Style Prosody." *Harvard Journal of Asiatic Studies*, Vol. 51, No. 2 (Dec. 1991).

Mair, Victor H. "Xie He's 'Six Laws' of Painting and Their Indian Parallels," in Zong-qi Cai, ed., *Chinese Aesthetics: The Ordering of Literature, the Arts, and the Universe in the Six Dynasties* (Honolulu: University of Hawai'i Press). 2004.

Mitter, Partha. *Art and Nationalism in Colonial India 1850-1922: Occidental Orientations*. Cambridge: Cambridge University Press. 1994.

Pollock, Sheldon. *The Language of the Gods in the World of Men: Sanskrit,*

Culture, and Power in Premodern India (Ranikhet: Permanent Black, 2007).

Ray, Paul and Anderson, Sherry Ruth. *Cultural Creatives: How 50 Million People are Changing the World*. New York: Three Rivers Press. 2000.

Said, Edward W. *Orientalism*. New York: Vintage. 1979.

Sri Aurobindo, The Life Divine, *CWSA Vol. 21 &22*. Pondicherry: Sri Aurobindo Ashram. 2005.

Sri Aurobindo, The Synthesis of Yoga, *CWSA Vol. 23 &24*. Pondicherry: Sri Aurobindo Ashram. 1999.

Sri Aurobindo, The Human Cycle, The Ideal of Human Unity, War and Self-Determination, *CWSA Vol. 25*. Pondicherry: Sri Aurobindo Ashram. 1997.

Sri Aurobindo, Savitri, *CWSA Vol. 33 and 34*. Pondicherry: Sri Aurobindo Ashram. 1997.

Tagore, Rabindranath. "Samudra Jatra," *Rabindra Rachanabali, Volume 13*, pp. 39-40, 1893.

Willis, Michael. *The Archeology of Hindu Ritual: Temples and the Establishment of the Gods*. New York: Cambridge University Press. 2009.

Introduction to *The Seasons*
Richard Hartz
Kalidasa and World Literature

Since the end of the eighteenth century when translations of *Shakuntala* began to circulate in Europe, captivating Goethe and others, Kalidasa has been assured of a place in global culture. India's foremost classical poet and dramatist has gradually become recognized as an author with whom a decently educated person anywhere on earth might be expected to have at least a nodding acquaintance. When Goethe in his later years announced the coming of an age of *Weltliteratur*, the world literature of which he spoke was still a radical new concept.[1] Today we take the idea for granted, but its content goes on evolving, expanding and diversifying.

We know almost nothing about Kalidasa's life except the little that can be gleaned from legends and inferences. Most scholars, however, associate him with the reign of Chandragupta II, who ruled over a substantial part of the Indian subcontinent in the late fourth and early fifth centuries. India was then at its peak of prosperity, creativity and influence. As a writer of Sanskrit, Kalidasa had access to a reading public that was perhaps the largest in the world. The "Sanskrit cosmopolis" described by Sheldon Pollock was constituted by the literary culture that spread across much of South and Southeast Asia, from present-day Afghanistan to Java, in the first millennium CE.[2] During the same period, Buddhism travelled to China and elsewhere, transmitting other aspects of

---

1 **Notes**
 "Nationalliteratur will jetzt nicht viel sagen, die Epoche der Weltliteratur ist an der Zeit, und jeder muß jetzt dazu wirken, diese Epoche zu beschleunigen." ("Nowadays, national literature doesn't mean much; the age of world literature is at hand and everyone should work to hasten its advent.") Conversation of 31 January 1827 in Johann Peter Eckermann, *Gespräche mit Goethe in den Letzten Jahren Seines Lebens*, ed. Fritz Bergemann (Baden-Baden: Insel Verlag, 1987), p. 211.
2 Sheldon Pollock, *The Language of the Gods in the World of Men: Sanskrit, Culture, and Power in Premodern India* (Ranikhet: Permanent Black, 2007).

India's intellectual and aesthetic culture in the process. The ancient world was more interconnected than we usually think. Kalidasa can be situated not only in the classical civilization of India which is brilliantly reflected in his writings, but in the larger context of the Asia of that era.

Kalidasa speaks to us of a world long vanished, yet strangely familiar. He appeals to universal aspects of human experience in ways that express the Indian or, more broadly, Asian sensibility of his time. His was a culture that knew the art of enjoying life. Nowhere is this more evident than in the work reproduced, translated and illustrated in this book. *Ṛtusaṁhāra*, "The Seasons," throbs from beginning to end with the sheer pleasure of living. It is clearly the composition of a young poet and is generally assumed to be Kalidasa's first. Critics point out signs of artistic immaturity. But the spirit of youth that breathes through it gives it an attraction of its own. Metrically and stylistically simpler than most of Kalidasa's other writings, it is in some ways easier to translate. Modest in scope and manner, its attribution to Kalidasa has even been thought to detract from his reputation and its authenticity has occasionally been questioned. Yet it continues to be read and enjoyed, translated and retranslated.

The fact that Kalidasa wrote in Sanskrit (and, in his plays, Prakrit) no longer guarantees him a large readership even in India. Like most of world literature, his works depend on translations to reach the global audience they deserve. But no translation, especially of poetry, can be a perfect substitute for the original. Much of the beauty of Kalidasa's writings seems destined to be lost to the vast majority of readers today. Yet the number of new translations published in recent years shows a continuing interest in the attempt to provide, as far as possible, substitutes in other languages for reading Kalidasa in the original. It is in the spirit of such an attempt that Bengali and English translations of *Ṛtusaṁhāra* are presented along with the Sanskrit text in this illustrated volume.

The Seasons and the Cosmic Order

Few things are as universal in human life as the experience of time's passage through an annually recurring series of changes in our natural environment. The number, names and characteristics of the seasons differ depending on where we are on the planet. Their regularity may be disturbed, as we now know all too well. But participation in the cycle of these moods of Nature has been a perennial feature of earthly existence. What has varied even more than their objective features is how we interpret and value this dimension of our lives. Interwoven with other aspects of culture, attitudes to the seasons have ranged at various times and places from religious or philosophical to sensuous and aesthetic to scientific or merely pragmatic.

In India, the oldest texts reveal a mentality far from the disenchanted modern worldview. The world was felt to be more alive. Meaning was ascribed to what we commonly take to be mechanical phenomena. The Sanskrit word for season, *ṛtu*, is closely related to the central Vedic concept of *ṛta*, the cosmic order. As Jeanine Miller explains, "*ṛta* concerns the *dynamics of manifestation*, the process of world unfoldment at all levels."[3] V. Raghavan clarifies the connection of the word for season with the more general word for the principle underlying the orderliness and regularity of all cosmic processes:

> *Ṛtu* and *ṛta* go together as two aspects of action or movement from the same root '*ṛ*' 'to go'.... While *ṛta* was the abstract aspect, *ṛtu* was the active aspect. It is from these ideas that *ṛtu* came to mean the form in which Nature expressed itself in an orderly sequence in particular, specific and patent forms, in short, the Seasons.[4]

---

3   Jeanine Miller, *The Vision of Cosmic Order in the Vedas* (London: Routledge & Kegan Paul, 1985), p. 38.
4   V. Raghavan, *Ṛtu in Sanskrit Literature* (Delhi: Shri Lal Bahadur Shastri Rashtriya Sanskrit Vidyapeetha, 2009), p. 1.

An Upanishad goes so far as to declare seasonality to be the very essence of the human condition: *ṛtur asmy ārtavo 'smi*, "Season am I, seasonal am I."[5] Raimundo Panikkar comments:

> Man is time, this text is saying, but not an empty time or a mere flow of the elements of his being. Man is temporal, "seasonal" (*ārtava*), inasmuch as he is a part of the cosmic order (*ṛta*) that is manifested in the annual cycle of the seasons (*ṛtu*).[6]

The antique religious imagination sometimes took strange forms. The Vedic *Puruṣa Sūkta* describes the genesis of the world through the sacrifice of a single thousand-headed, thousand-eyed, thousand-footed Person (*puruṣa*) from the parts of whose body all things were formed. In this cosmogenic ritual, "the primeval spirit, instead of remaining one, homogeneous whole, was fragmented into the many forms pervaded by the one life, its own life-breath."[7] The seasons played a key role in this primeval diversifying event: spring (*vasanta*) was the clarified butter, summer (*grīṣma*) the fuel, autumn (*śarad*) the oblation.[8] In a variant, the water of the rainy season (*prāvṛṣ*) is also sprinkled.[9] Elsewhere in the Vedic literature, winter (*hemanta*) is mentioned as well and the seasons are counted as five. Later the dewy season (*śiśira*) is distinguished from winter proper and placed after it.

Thus the year came to be divided into the two-month periods regarded as the six seasons of the year throughout the subsequent Indian tradition.[10] Long after the Vedas, Kalidasa inherited this calendar and celebrated it in poetry of a refined sensuality expressing a view of life and art belonging to a later age. Yet continuities remained in the vision of a harmonious

---

5 *Kauṣītaki Upaniṣad* 1.2.
6 Raimundo Panikkar, *The Vedic Experience: Mantramañjarī, An Anthology of the Vedas for Modern Man and Contemporary Celebration* (Pondicherry: All India Books, 1983), p. 787.
7 Miller, *The Vision of Cosmic Order in the Vedas*, p. 205.
8 Ṛgveda 10.90.6.
9 Atharvaveda 19.6.11.
10 Raghavan, *Ṛtu in Sanskrit Literature*, p. 2.

world pulsating with the rhythms of a spirit whose hidden presence the poet strives to make us feel.

Soma, Ananda and Rasa

The Vedic poet was one who was gifted with insight into the mysteries behind the appearances of things. His inspired words sprang from an illumined intoxication of the spirit accessible only to the *kavi*, meaning originally a seer as well as a poet. *Soma*, the god of ecstasy, presided over this supernaturally elevated state. In the course of time, the concrete symbolism of the Vedic religion evolved into the more abstract and impersonal intuitions of the Upanishads. Out of the practices and experiences associated with *Soma* developed the philosophical conception or spiritual realization of *ānanda*, the bliss underlying all that is. "For who could live or breathe," asks the *Taittiriya Upaniṣad*,[11] "if there were not this delight of existence as the ether in which we dwell?"[12]

We breathe this atmosphere, Vedanta tells us, yet rarely feel it in its purity because ordinarily our desires and aversions distort our response. Far from being inherently blissful, life may even seem more painful than pleasurable. But in one domain, at least, the contrary is true. Aesthetic experience, as Sri Aurobindo observes, "admits us in one part of our nature to that detachment from egoistic sensation and that universal attitude through which the one Soul sees harmony and beauty where we divided beings experience rather chaos and discord."[13]

Indian aesthetics based itself on this discovery. To designate its central concept, it adopted another word which occurs in the Upanishads in connection with *ānanda*: the term *rasa*.[14] From the basic ideas of sap,

---

11 *Taittirīya Upaniṣad* 2.7: *ko hyevānyāt kaḥ prāṇyāt, yad eṣa ākāśa ānando na syāt.*
12 Sri Aurobindo, *The Life Divine* (Pondicherry: Sri Aurobindo Ashram, 2005), p. 98.
13 Ibid., p. 117.
14 *Rasa* is explicitly connected with *ānanda* in *Taittirīya Upaniṣad* 2.7, where the sentence already quoted follows a statement that one who seizes the *rasa* (the taste

essence and taste, *rasa* came to refer to a quintessence of feeling that can be extracted from emotions in which our personal interests are not entangled. Negative as well as positive emotions can be so transmuted. This sublimation which is normally difficult to achieve in life comes naturally, Sri Aurobindo points out, to the aesthetic consciousness:

> We attain to something of this capacity for variable but universal delight in the aesthetic reception of things as represented by Art and Poetry, so that we enjoy there the Rasa or taste of the sorrowful, the terrible, even the horrible or repellent; and the reason is because we are detached, disinterested, not thinking of ourselves or of self-defence (*jugupsā*), but only of the thing and its essence.[15]

As an aesthetic term, *rasa* denotes a superior form of pleasure to which it is claimed that the arts can give access. In the plural, the *rasas* are various modifications of this essence of aesthetic emotion corresponding to the feelings, pleasant or unpleasant in themselves, from which *rasa* can be elicited. As M. Hiriyanna observes, "*Rasa* is, in its intrinsic nature, but *one* . . . and its so-called varieties are only different forms of it, due to a difference in their respective psychological determinants. In its fundamental character, it signifies a mood of emotional exaltation. . . ."[16]

Rasa theory emerged alongside the development of poetry, drama and other arts during the centuries leading up to and following Kalidasa. Originally applied mainly to drama, the idea of *rasa* with its variations arising from the transformation of ordinary emotions was elaborated into a distinctive contribution of Indian aesthetics in general. Some theorists, as Pollock observes, brought a Vedantic perspective to the

---

of the essence of things) becomes full of *ānanda* (*rasaṁ hyevāyaṁ labdhvānandī bhavati*).
15 Sri Aurobindo, *The Life Divine*, pp. 116–17.
16 M. Hiriyanna, "Art Experience," in Nalini Bhushan and Jay L. Garfield, eds., *Indian Philosophy in English: From Renaissance to Independence* (New York: Oxford University Press, 2011), p. 227.

conception of *rasa* "as the experience of consciousness itself, when consciousness is thoroughly evacuated of the dross of everyday life so as to become, as it were, self-transcendent." The seventeenth century thinker Vishvanathadeva, in particular, "authorizes this view by citing the *Taittirīya Upaniṣad*'s ancient doctrine that the self is composed of five sheaths, the last of which is the 'bliss component.' This component is naturally obscured by the processes of phenomenal life, but in aesthetic experience, given the peculiar nature of its revelation, everything that conceals the bliss that is consciousness is removed: the 'veil of unknowing is lifted.' "[17]

By the classical age of Indian civilization, the poet (*kavi*) had lost the hieratic function of his Vedic predecessors. Yet by imparting the experience of *rasa* to his cultivated audience, he could still communicate a kind of rapture uplifted beyond mundane preoccupations. Kalidasa is the consummate *kavi* in this sense. His early work on the seasons, even if not ranked among his masterpieces, is in many ways a thoroughly Kalidasian composition exuding *rasa* from every verse. It can serve as an accessible introduction to Sanskrit poetry and is, besides, an important treatment of a major theme of literature and art not only in India, but elsewhere in Asia.

The Seasons and the Way of Heaven

Cultural evolution in different parts of Asia proceeded partly on independent or diverging, partly on parallel or converging lines. The easily observable contrasts are only part of the picture. Some similarities or convergences can be explained as due to common origins or transmission of influences; others remain unexplained. From this point of view, the role of the seasons in Asian art and culture is a topic that has

---

17 Sheldon Pollock, ed. and trans., *A Rasa Reader: Classical Indian Aesthetics* (New York: Columbia University Press, 2016), pp. 24–25.

yet to be adequately explored. For the purpose of this introduction, a few observations will suffice for now to enlarge our view of the subject to include China as well as India.

In ancient China, as in India, we find the cycle of the seasons regarded from the earliest times as a deeply significant manifestation of a universal order. The "Spring and Autumn" period of Chinese history, from the eighth to the fifth century BCE, received its name from the *Spring and Autumn Annals*, a chronicle traditionally ascribed to Confucius himself. It has been suggested that spring and autumn in the title of this classic represent "the continuous rise and fall of ruling houses."[18] Perhaps, but there is more to it than that. In a related text attributed to the second century BCE Confucian scholar Dong Zhongshu, recently translated and published as *Luxuriant Gems of the Spring and Autumn*, the seasons are introduced in a section on the conduct of public affairs and how it should reflect the Way of Heaven:

> I have heard that the standards adopted by the sage-kings were modeled on the great warp of Heaven, which completes each season with three months and each year with four [seasonal] revolutions. . . . According completely with Heaven's numbers to assist in [the conduct of] human affairs signifies that government carefully attends to the Way.[19]

The attributes of the seasons are interpreted in this text in terms of the complementarity of yin and yang as applied to both psychology and cosmology. If we recall the Vedic view of human beings as fundamentally "seasonal" in their manner of expressing the cosmic order, we seem to encounter here the Chinese version of a similar conception:

---

18 Stephen Owen, ed., *The Cambridge History of Chinese Literature*, vol. 1 (Cambridge, UK: Cambridge University Press, 2011), p. 46.
19 Sarah A. Queen and John S. Major, ed. and trans., *Luxuriant Gems of the Spring and Autumn* (New York: Columbia University Press, 2016), pp. 257–58.

Spring is the loving will;
summer is the joyous will;
autumn is the stern will;
winter is the sorrowful will.
Therefore to love and yet know sternness, to be joyous and yet know sorrow, are the regulations of the four seasons. . . .

The yang of spring and summer and the yin of autumn and winter do not reside in Heaven alone. They also reside in human beings. . . .

Therefore it is said: Heaven surely possesses expressions of happiness, anger, sorrow, and joy, and human beings likewise possess the *qi* of spring, autumn, winter, and summer.[20]

Elsewhere in the *Luxuriant Gems*, late summer is added as another distinct season. This allows the seasons to be correlated with the five "elements" of Chinese thought: wood, fire, earth, metal and water.[21] The Five-Phase cosmology is connected in turn with the "five affairs" (expression, speech, sight, hearing, thought) which manifest "the destiny that human beings receive from Heaven."[22]

Some of these ideas have survived into the present in aspects of Chinese culture such as traditional medicine and Taoism. Recently they have even been popularized outside of China, sometimes combined with borrowings from the Indian tradition. Contemporary interest is motivated by the sense of a lost harmony with nature that needs to be recovered, as can be seen in this passage from a book on "Hatha and Taoist yoga for the seasons":

> There is no doubt that energy moves through us differently according to the time of day, the climatic conditions, the attitudes we harbor and the cycles of the moon, just to name a few. With the natural flow of seasons, so too it makes sense that our yoga practice is to reflect these changes. Throughout Chinese medicine

---
20 Ibid., pp. 407–8.
21 Ibid., pp. 442–43.
22 Ibid., p. 488.

and Taoist thought, the aim is to find and establish harmony by aligning with the natural flow of life.... These ideas are not limited to Chinese thought and can be found throughout Ayurvedic medicine (said to be the oldest medicine on the planet), yogic science and many other traditions and cultures who place great importance on learning from the changes in nature.[23]

Some resemblances between Chinese medicine and the Indian system of Ayurveda are indeed striking. Like other similarities between the two cultures, they may have come about partly through direct contact. Victor Mair, speaking of "the massive impact of Buddhism on Chinese culture during the Six Dynasties, the Sui, and the Tang," observes parenthetically:

Certainly, Buddhism was the main vehicle for the transmission of all sorts of Indian cultural elements to China during this period, but it was not the sole vehicle, nor was all that it brought specifically Buddhist in nature (e.g., mathematics, medicine, linguistics, prosody, and countless stories, to name just a few important areas of Chinese culture in which fundamental changes occurred as a result of the importation of Indian ideas and techniques).[24]

Transmissions that pertain directly to Buddhism have so far been studied a good deal more thoroughly than those that do not. With regard to the latter, much may remain still to be discovered. Our present subject, poetry on the seasons in the classical literatures, is one whose surface has only to be scratched to yield tantalizing parallels which might merit further investigation.

---

23 Michael Hetherington, *The Complete Book of Oriental Yoga: Hatha and Taoist Yoga for the Seasons* (Mind Heart Publishing, 2014), p. 11.
24 Victor H. Mair, "Xie He's 'Six Laws' of Painting and Their Indian Parallels," in Zong-qi Cai, ed., *Chinese Aesthetics: The Ordering of Literature, the Arts, and the Universe in the Six Dynasties* (Honolulu: University of Hawai'i Press, 2004), p. 97.

Kalidasa's *Seasons* and *Midnight Songs*

As archaic religio-philosophical interpretations of the seasonal cycle receded into the background in Asia's oldest cultures, the growing secular literatures became vehicles for the expression of richly aesthetic and hedonistic responses to Nature's moods. It is in this spirit that Kalidasa approached the seasons. Sri Aurobindo identifies what it is in *Ṛtusaṁhāra* that, despite artistic defects presumably due to the young poet's inexperience, nevertheless vindicates it as Kalidasa's own:

> Especially is it significant in its daring gift of sensuousness. The prophet of a hedonistic civilisation here seizes with no uncertain hand on the materials of his work.[25]

Summing up the character of what is often called the classical age of Indian culture, best represented in literature by Kalidasa, Sri Aurobindo describes its relationship to what preceded and followed:

> The grand basic principles and lines of Indian religion, philosophy, society have already been found and built and the steps of the culture move now in the magnitude and satisfying security of a great tradition; but there is still ample room for creation and discovery within these fields and a much wider province, great beginnings, strong developments of science and art and literature, the freedom of the purely intellectual and aesthetic activities, much scope too for the hedonisms of the vital and the refinements of the emotional being, a cultivation of the art and rhythmic practice of life.

Drawing an implied contrast with the debauchery allegedly rampant in the declining Roman Empire during roughly the same period, Sri Aurobindo continues:

> There is a highly intellectualised vital stress and a many-sided interest in living, an indulgence of an at once intellectual and

---

25 Sri Aurobindo, *Early Cultural Writings* (Pondicherry: Sri Aurobindo Ashram, 2003), p. 185.

vital and sensuous satisfaction extending even to a frankness of physical and sensual experience, but in the manner of the oriental mind with a certain decorousness and order, an element of aesthetic restraint and the observance of rule and measure even in indulgence that saves always from the unbridled licence to which less disciplined races are liable.[26]

Around the time when Kalidasa was writing about the seasons in India, intriguingly similar poetry on this topic was being composed in China. *Midnight Songs of the Four Seasons*, traditionally ascribed to the elusive "Lady Midnight," is dated to the latter half of the fourth century CE during the politically unstable but culturally fruitful period of the Six Dynasties. It resembles and differs from Kalidasa's contemporaneous work in ways that can help to bring into sharper focus the distinctive features of *Ṛtusaṁhāra* as an example not only of classical Sanskrit poetry, but of wider trends in Asian literature.

We know, if anything, even less about Lady Midnight than we do about Kalidasa. As the translator David Hinton remarks, here "we find ourselves in that shadowy realm between the anonymous oral tradition and individual authorship."[27] The most salient characteristic of these lyrics is the female voice heard in them, presumed to be that of a professional entertainer.[28] Her dialect, Mair observes, "was of southeast China, a region known for its women poets."[29] Otherwise, the treatment of the

---

26 Sri Aurobindo, *The Renaissance in India and Other Essays on Indian Culture* (Pondicherry: Sri Aurobindo Ashram, 2004), p. 356.
27 David Hinton, trans. and ed., *Classical Chinese Poetry: An Anthology* (New York: Farrar, Straus and Giroux, 2008), p. 73.
28 The poetess's likely profession is discussed in the introduction to Lenore Mayhew and William McNaughton, trs., *A Gold Orchid: The Love Poems of Tzu Yeh* (Ruthland, Vt.: Charles E. Tuttle, 1972). Putting forward the theory that she was a "wine-shop girl" and clarifying the exact nature of that occupation, the translators claim that this "would account for the subjects and scenes of which she writes, and would explain (which is less easy) her considerable poetic skill."
29 Victor H. Mair, ed., *The Shorter Columbia Anthology of Traditional Chinese Literature* (New York: Columbia University Press, 2000), p. 253. Although women

theme is surprisingly similar to Kalidasa's in a number of ways. Both bodies of verse show less interest in describing Nature from the outside than in registering the impact of her changing phases on the human mind, heart and senses. Particularly, both the Sanskrit and the Chinese poems focus on how the seasons affect the feelings and behavior of lovers. In the language of Indian poetics, the dominant *rasa* in *Ṛtusaṁhāra* and *Midnight Songs* alike is *śṛṅgāra*, in which romantic love and sensuous passion are sublimated into the more detached enjoyment of aesthetic emotion.

When we compare the original texts, what strikes us first is their formal resemblances. Both consist of stanzas of four lines each with an equal number of syllables in every line. The stanza is a complete artistic unit, a poem or song that can stand by itself, like a miniature painting. Sri Aurobindo's observations about this form would be almost equally applicable to *Midnight Songs*, apart from the Sanskrit terminology:

> The unit of this poetical art is the *śloka*, the sufficient verse of four quarters or *pādas*, and each *śloka* is expected to be a work of perfect art in itself, a harmonious, vivid and convincing expression of an object, scene, detail, thought, sentiment, state of mind or emotion that can stand by itself as an independent figure. . . . It is this carefully artistic and highly cultured type of poetic creation that reached its acme of perfection in the poetry of Kalidasa.[30]

The five-character quatrain employed throughout *Midnight Songs of the Four Seasons* can be illustrated by the first poem in the collection:

---

poets tended to be overshadowed by men everywhere in the ancient world, they existed in India as well as China. As Dr. Raghavan points out, it is "from the Anthologies that we know of the poetesses of the classical age" (*Ṛtu in Sanskrit Literature*, p. 119).

30 Sri Aurobindo, *The Renaissance in India*, p. 358.

春风动春心，
流目瞩山林。
山林多奇采，
阳鸟吐清音。

chūn fēng dòng chūn xīn,
liú mù zhǔ shān lín.
shān lín duō qí cǎi,
yáng niǎo tǔ qīng yīn.

Word-for-word translation:

(The) spring wind move(s) (the) spring heart (i.e., stirs romantic feelings),
wander(ing) eye(s) gaze (at the) mountain forest.
(The) mountain forest (is) so wonderful(ly) splendid,
sun(ny) bird(s) pour clear sound.

We find a similar association of ideas and images in a *śloka* of Kalidasa on the spring wind. Here there are fourteen syllables in each line, arranged in a complex pattern of long and short:

आकम्पयन्कुसुमिताः सहकारशाखा
विस्तारयन्परभृतस्य वचांसि दिक्षु ।
वायुर्विवाति हृदयानि हरन्नराणां
नीहारपातविगमात्सुभगो वसन्ते ॥

ākampayan kusumitāḥ sahakāra-śākhā
vistārayan parabhṛtasya vacāṁsi dikṣu,
vāyur vivāti hṛdayāni haran narāṇāṁ
nīhāra-pāta-vigamāt subhago vasante.

Literal translation:
Shaking the flowering mango branches,
spreading the cuckoo's calls in all directions,
the wind blows stealing the hearts of men,
because of dew-fall's departure enjoyable in spring.

The key correspondence between Kalidasa's stanza and its Chinese counterpart is between the lines where "wind" and "heart" occur: wind moving or stirring the heart in the first line of the Chinese, wind stealing or capturing hearts in the third line of the Sanskrit. Trees and birds fill out the picture in each case, bird-calls adding an auditory dimension to the visual and tactile experiences evoked.

Detailed parallels aside, what these depictions have in common is the sensory vividness of the scene each brings before the mind with a few strokes. The unique compression of Chinese poetry cannot be equaled in Sanskrit with its polysyllabic vocabulary. When Sanskrit compounds are dissolved, however, the number of words in each line is approximately the same. Another linguistic contrast has to do with the role of grammatical terminations in specifying the precise relations between Sanskrit words. In Chinese, as Hinton observes, "grammatical elements are minimal in the extreme, allowing a remarkable openness and ambiguity that leaves a great deal unstated."[31] Sanskrit poetry at its best also suggests much more than is overtly stated, but it does so in another way and with a resonant word-music of its own.

Sanskrit meters cannot be duplicated in any other language, but a translation that gives no sense of the rhythmic vitality of the original fails to convey an important aspect of it. In freely rendering Kalidasa's lines, besides reproducing the essential imagery and sensory stimuli they represent, I have tried to catch an echo of their exuberant rhythm using the metrical resources available in English:

---

31 Hinton, *Classical Chinese Poetry*, pp. xx–xxi.

Rioting in the movement of the mango boughs,
Spreading abroad the cuckoo's call, the winds carouse,
Delightful in the season when the dews depart,
Quickening with their warm embrace the throbbing heart.

Indian and Chinese Poetry in the Silk Road Era

Specific resemblances between Kalidasa's lines and Chinese verses on the same subject probably did not come about through direct borrowing in either direction, yet they raise questions that are worth looking into. Almost identical associations of ideas and images – in the above instance, spring-wind-trees-birds-heart – could have suggested themselves independently to poets in unconnected locations. But similar aesthetic cultures would be most likely to select similar elements of experience as suitable material for poetic treatment. However it happened, the literary traditions of India and China had evidently developed significant affinities by the time the seasons emerged as a major topic for poetry.

In the first millennium CE, much of Eurasia was linked together, however loosely, by the Silk Road. If only for this reason, it may be worth taking a fresh look at Kalidasa in a context extending well beyond India. Silk itself, mentioned in *Ṛtusaṁhāra* in almost every one of the six seasons, owed its prominence to the diffusion of sericulture and export of silk from China. The Gupta rulers, Xinru Liu notes, "inherited a taste for rare commodities from abroad, and thereby sustained the market for the luxurious goods the Silk Road trade provided." She goes on:

> Literature, art, and architecture all represented the refined lifestyle of the Gupta elite, and among the fineries they most enjoyed were the silk textiles from China. The Gupta Empire, like other sedentary states, had also established its own silk weaving industry. India had its own indigenous species of silkworm, but

it differed from those the Chinese used. . . . Chinese silk textiles remained the most coveted.³²

In the last year of the fourth century, the Buddhist pilgrim Faxian set out on foot from China for India across some of the most forbidding deserts and mountains in the world. After his return fourteen years later, he wrote an account of his travels which, though narrowly focused on topics related to Buddhism, seems to have contributed to a growing Chinese perception of India as a flourishing and culturally advanced society. As Tansen Sen remarks: "Faxian's work triggered a wider discussion among Chinese intellectuals about Indic culture and society vis-à-vis the Sinitic civilization, a dialogue that continued through to the twentieth century."³³

Faxian made his epic journey during the reign of Chandragupta II, the probable time of Kalidasa. His *Record of the Buddhist Kingdoms* contains little information about non-Buddhist aspects of Indian culture, but it stands as a reminder that, whatever geographical barriers separated them, the two most ancient civilizations of Asia were not unrelated worlds. Sometimes the connections show up in unexpected ways. Despite the phonological disparity between Chinese and Sanskrit, for example, it has been demonstrated that Chinese attempts to emulate the metrical system of Buddhist Sanskrit texts led to the formulation of the rules of tonal prosody of Recent Style verse, which became the favored poetic form of the Tang dynasty (618–907 CE).³⁴

A couple of centuries before the Tang era, the pentasyllabic quatrains of *Midnight Songs* had anticipated an important feature of Recent Style prosody. Mair and Mei mention the four-*pāda* structure of the Sanskrit

---

32 Xinru Liu, *The Silk Road in World History* (New York: Oxford University Press, 2010), p. 84.
33 Tansen Sen, India, China, and the World: A Connected History (Lanham, MD: Rowman & Littlefield, 2017), p. 50.
34 Victor H. Mair and Tsu-Lin Mei, "The Sanskrit Origins of Recent Style Prosody," *Harvard Journal of Asiatic Studies*, Vol. 51, No. 2 (Dec. 1991).

śloka as a factor in "the emergence of the quatrain as a basic module of composition" in Recent Style poetry.[35] But elsewhere Mair notes that this trend had already been foreshadowed in *Midnight Songs*, whose impact he acknowledges: "As witty, fluent examples of the five-syllable quatrain form, they had a significant influence on the poetry of ensuing centuries."[36]

Based on our present knowledge, we must take the structural resemblance between the quatrains of *Midnight Songs* and the *ślokas* of Kalidasa to be coincidental. But if this assumption ends up being reconsidered in the light of new evidence, it will not be the first time such a revision has occurred. To cite an example from the visual arts, the numerical similarity between Xie He's "Six Laws" of painting in Chinese art and the "Six Limbs" of Indian art theory was regarded as coincidental for almost a century after Abanindranath Tagore first pointed it out in 1914. Only rather recently has Mair shown by a detailed examination of the two systems that the Six Laws, which date to the early sixth century CE, exhibit such precise and numerous correspondences in form and content to the Six Limbs, whose origins probably go back at least a century or two earlier, that "it is virtually impossible that they are unrelated." His conclusion may well be applicable to as yet unexplored instances of "the intricate interplay between external influences and internal dynamics":

> The identical process that occurred with regard to the evolution of Sanskrit prosodic rules into the standards governing regulated verse in China transpired with the transformation of the Six Limbs into the Six Laws. They started out as a product of India and became a naturalized cultural manifestation of China. Neither the rules governing prosody nor the principles regulating painting were identifiably Buddhist, but they were conveyed to

---

35 Ibid., p. 382.
36 Mair, *The Shorter Columbia Anthology*, p. 253.

China primarily by Buddhists and were certainly fostered within Chinese Buddhist circles of laymen and monks.[37]

The modifications such influences undergo in another cultural context, among other factors, make the process of transmission difficult to trace. When the receiving culture so thoroughly adapts what it takes in or responds to, it may be more appropriate to speak of stimulation than borrowing. The result, in any case, is the interweaving of neighboring cultures with marked individualities, but equally pronounced affinities.

The Philosophy of the Seasons in Asian Literatures

By the time of Kalidasa, as we have seen, cultural developments in India and China had converged in certain ways to produce, at times, curiously similar treatments even of themes with no obvious connection to Buddhism. The undoubted impact of Buddhism on the representation of nature in Chinese poetry occurred later and took a different form. Beginning in the Tang period, as Prabodh Chandra Bagchi points out, Buddhist thought with its "notion of universal impermanence, had an abiding influence on the poets and artists and influenced the Chinese esthetic outlook." A consciousness of "the fleeting nature of everything"[38] often found artistic expression through imagery drawn from the mutations of the seasons.

Moreover, it is at least partly due to the transmission of Buddhist thought from China through Korea to Japan that, as Haruo Shirane observes, Japanese poetry also "displays extreme sensitivity to the transience of nature and the passing of the seasons.... Natural change

---

37 Mair, "Xie He's 'Six Laws' of Painting and Their Indian Parallels," pp. 110–11.
38 Prabodh Chandra Bagchi, "Indian Influence on Chinese Thought," in Bangwei Wang and Tansen Sen, eds., *India and China: Interactions through Buddhism and Diplomacy. A Collection of Essays by Professor Prabodh Chandra Bagchi* (Delhi: Anthem Press, 2011), p. 41.

came to be a metaphor for the transience of life and the uncertainties of this world, a view that was reinforced by the Buddhist belief in the evanescence of all things." He adds:

> This perspective became particularly prominent from the Heian period (794–1185) and permeates poetic representations of both nature and human life, as exemplified by such a seasonal topic as cherry blossoms, which scatter as soon as they bloom.[39]

But impermanence is not all that the seasons represent. There is also their complementary aspect of regular recurrence – though it can no longer be taken for granted as much as it used to be.[40] In India, as well as in China and Japan before the depiction of the seasons underwent Buddhist influence, this more positive significance predominated in poetry celebrating the natural, socio-political and metaphysical order as a background or stimulant to human life and love. Contrary to the spiritually liberating but potentially life-discouraging Buddhist notion of an emptiness at the heart of things, the Vedic vision was profoundly world-affirming. Raghavan brings out the deeper assumptions that could be seen as implicit in the treatment of the seasons in Indian poetry:

---

39 Haruo Shirane, *Japan and the Culture of the Four Seasons: Nature, Literature, and the Arts* (New York: Columbia University Press, 2012), p. 133.

40 "Even transience is mutating," laments the anonymous author of a recent article on the impact of climate change on Japanese poets, who by tradition are expected to include a *kigo* or seasonal word with appropriate emotional associations in every haiku. "But as the climate warms and weather becomes more extreme," the article observes, "*kigo* are slipping from their seasonal moorings." Cherry blossoms, a prime example, "have long provoked reflections on beauty, transience and the unceasing rhythms of the natural world. This year, their [premature] annual appearance has many thinking about how those rhythms are changing" ("Another species harmed by climate change: Japanese poets," *The Economist – Asia Edition*, April 8, 2021, accessed May 22, 2021, https://www.economist.com/asia/ 2021/04/08/another-species-harmed-by-climate-change-japanese-poets).

Vedānta Deśika gave a philosophical turn to this idea that all seasons are aspects of Time, being expressions of the all-comprehensive Supreme Being.... Although not in so many express theological terms, it is this mystic idea that is behind all the descriptions of seasons in Sanskrit literature. When Sanskrit poetry describes all *Ṛtus* with equal fervour ... it is the realisation of this One ultimate all-comprehensive Being, which is also the fountain-head of Beauty and the basis of all expressions of Beauty, that fills the heart of the poet and suffuses all his expression; this is the philosophy of *Ṛtu-Kāvya* [season- poetry].[41]

It is in the poetry of Kalidasa – not only in *Ṛtusaṁhāra*, but wherever in his writings the seasons figure – that this philosophy of the seasons is most perfectly embodied. In an essay on translating Kalidasa found among Sri Aurobindo's early manuscripts, he links Kalidasa's sensuality itself, most conspicuous in *The Seasons*, to the seemingly opposite spiritual tendency for which India is known:

This, I think, is the essential attraction which makes his countrymen to this day feel such a passionate delight in Kalidasa; after reading a poem of his the world and life and our fellow creatures human, animal or inanimate have become suddenly more beautiful and dear to us than they were before; the heart flows out towards birds and beasts and the very trees seem to be drawing us towards them with their branches as if with arms.... Our own common thoughts, feelings and passions have also become suddenly fair to us; they have received the sanction of beauty. And then through the passion of delight and the sense of life and of love in all beautiful objects we reach to the Mighty Spirit behind them whom our soul recognizes no longer as an

---

41 Raghavan, *Ṛtu in Sanskrit Literature*, pp. 134–35.

object of knowledge or of worship but as her lover. . . . Thus by a singular paradox, one of those beautiful oxymorons of which the Hindu temperament is full, we reach God through the senses.[42]

---

[42] Sri Aurobindo, *Early Cultural Writings*, pp. 215–16.

Note on the English Translation
Richard Hartz
Metrical Translation and Free Verse

The advent of free verse has had a dramatic impact on the way poetry is translated as well as the way it is written. Until early in the last century, translators of poetry commonly used meter and, when appropriate, rhyme to convey a sense of the formal properties of the original. While that practice has continued in recent versions of some of the classics of Western literature, it has all but disappeared in the case of English translations from Indian languages. Nor has prose, previously the normal alternative to metrical translation of poetry, been widely reverted to as the default medium.

Free verse, whatever it may be in theory, often enough amounts in practice to little more than prose cut up into irregular lines. Equipped with this accommodating technique and liberated from the exacting constraints of regular form, translators of poetry could be expected to perform their task more easily, accurately and reliably. But how free verse translations actually compare with the results of other approaches is an empirical question that can only be decided by looking at examples of each. In translating Kalidasa's *Ṛtusaṁhāra* in rhymed and metered stanzas, I have assumed that in the age of free verse there is still room for hazarding another solution – call it old or new – to the difficult problem of rendering Sanskrit poetry into English.

In the last few decades, the movement of New Formalism has shown that meter and rhyme have not been relegated irrevocably to the past by the free verse revolution.[1] Every revolution creates a new orthodoxy. Free verse seemed for a while to occupy that position both

---

1 **Notes**
Robert McPhillips, *The New Formalism: A Critical Introduction* (Cincinnati, OH: Textos Books, 2003).

for poets and for translators of poetry. But with a more open-minded attitude, translators are free to reconsider all the resources available in the target language and its literary traditions, including those that had perhaps prematurely been dismissed as obsolete.

Translation as Interpretation

Ideally, a translation should give the reader an experience as similar as possible to that of reading the original. David Bellos calls this finding a match:

> What translators do is find matches, not equivalences, for the units of which a work is made, in the hope and expectation that their sum will produce a new work that can serve overall as a substitute for the source. . . . No translation is the same as its source, and no translation can be expected to be like its source in more than a few selected ways. . . . If meaning and force are kept the same and if in a limited set of other respects a translation is seen to be like its source, then we have a match.[2]

In this complex process, it is hardly possible to pay equal attention to all aspects of the original at once. Choices have to be made. Bellos explains:

> By choosing which dimensions to connect in a relationship of likeness and the extent to which the likeness is made visible, a translation hierarchizes the interlocking, overlaying features of the original. To that extent at least, translations always provide an interpretation of the source.[3]

The interpretation of Kalidasa's *Seasons* that has inspired the present translation was influenced by Sri Aurobindo's view of Kalidasa as

---

2 David Bellos, *Is That a Fish in Your Ear? Translation and the Meaning of Everything* (New York: Faber and Faber, 2011), pp. 308, 322.
3 Ibid., p. 321.

preeminently a "poet of the senses, of aesthetic beauty, of sensuous emotion." More specifically, a "strong visualising faculty ... and the concrete presentation which this definiteness of vision demanded" constitute "the characteristic Kalidasian manner."[4] If so, Kalidasa could be ranked with the Chinese poets admired by Ezra Pound in terms of the quality Pound calls "phanopoeia", defined as "throwing the object (fixed or moving) on to the visual imagination." Phanopoeia is, according to Pound, one of the chief means by which poets can "charge language with meaning to the utmost possible degree." But like some of the ancient Greeks, Kalidasa also excels in the attribute for which Pound coined the term "melopoeia," defined by him as "inducing emotional correlations by the sound and rhythm of the speech."[5]

In translating *The Seasons*, I have made an effort to balance or, if possible, fuse these two dimensions, visual and auditory. While striving for vividness and precision in reproducing Kalidasa's imagery, I have sought at the same time to catch an echo of the "vigour, fire and force" felt by Sri Aurobindo to be the qualities animating his "splendid diction and versification."[6]

Literalness and Readability

An example will serve to illustrate how I have tried to achieve this combination. Kalidasa begins the cycle of the seasons unconventionally with the heat of the Indian summer so that he can conclude with a celebration of spring. In all six seasons, the *śṛṅgāra rasa* or amorous mood that pervades the poem is expressed primarily through depictions of the joy of union in various manifestations against Nature's kaleidoscopic background. But the passion of love only grows more intense when it

---

4 Sri Aurobindo, *Early Cultural Writings* (Pondicherry: Sri Aurobindo Ashram, 2003), pp. 162–63.
5 Ezra Pound, *ABC of Reading* (New York: New Directions, 2010), p. 63.
6 Sri Aurobindo, *Early Cultural Writings*, p. 185.

is subjected to hardship and starved of contact. We see this in the tenth stanza of "Summer," which reads in my translation:

> Blind with the dust that swirls across his way,
> The traveller endures two fires by day,
> His flesh afflicted by the sun above,
> His heart by separation from his love.

The original uses a meter called *vaṁśastha* with twelve syllables in each line, arranged in a sequence of long and short (‿ – ‿ – – ‿ ‿ – ‿ – ‿ –):

असह्यवातोद्धतरेणुमण्डला
प्रचण्डसूर्यातपतापिता मही ।
न शक्यते द्रष्टुमपि प्रवासिभिः
प्रियावियोगानलदग्धमानसैः ॥

asahya-vātoddhata-reṇu-maṇḍalā
pracaṇḍa-sūryātapa-tāpitā mahī,
na śakyate draṣṭum api pravāsibhiḥ
priyā-viyogānala-dagdha-mānasaiḥ.

In 1916, M. R. Kale published the Sanskrit text of *Ṛtusaṁhāra* with Sanskrit and English commentaries and a prose translation in English evidently intended to help students struggling through the original. His edition is valuable for that purpose, but his translation of this *śloka* also shows what happens when Sanskrit poetry is rendered literally:

> Travellers, whose hearts are scorched by the fire of separation from their sweethearts, cannot even look at the earth, wherein columns of dust are raised by unbearable gusts (of wind), (and) which is heated by the blaze of the fierce sun.[7]

---

[7] M. R. Kale, *The Ṛtusaṁhāra of Kālidāsa* (Delhi: Motilal Banarsidass, 1967), p. 78.

Judged by the criterion of word-for-word correspondence, Kale's translation is as good as any. Without altering the words, nowadays it could be turned into a semblance of free verse:

Travellers, whose hearts are scorched
by the fire of separation from their sweethearts,
cannot even look at the earth,
wherein columns of dust are raised
by unbearable gusts of wind,
and which is heated by the blaze
of the fierce sun.

Yet literal as his version is, Kale ignores not only the grammatical construction, which he has changed from passive to active, but the aesthetically significant feature of the order of the words and lines. Using mostly the same words, but putting them in the order of the Sanskrit and hyphenating its long compounds, we get this:

The unbearable-wind-raised-dust-swirling
fierce-sun-blaze-heated earth
cannot even be seen by travellers
with sweetheart-separation-fire-scorched hearts.

Although this suggests the forceful compactness of Kalidasa's style, unfortunately it is not English. All who venture to translate Sanskrit poetry would seem to face the problem of deciding where to position themselves on a scale from maximum literalness to maximum readability. To give an idea of how recent translators have responded to this challenge, here are four versions of the same stanza which have been published since the 1980s:

Hearts burning in the fire of separation,
men far from home can scarcely bear to see
the swirling clouds of dust tossed up
from the earth burnt by the sun's fierce heat. (Rajan)[8]

> Travellers, their hearts seared
> > by the fires of separation from their lovers,
> cannot see even the earth,
> > parched by the sun
> and obscured by whirls of dust
> > blown up by fierce winds. (Selby)[9]

Away in distant lands, the lovers miss their sweethearts.
With hearts singed by the fire of separation,
They are unable to face the dust storms that blow;
Nor even bear to look at
The cracked earth baked by intense heat. (Tandon)[10]

The wind may be unbearable,
so laden with dust it is;
the earth may be lying scorched
in the fierce blaze from the sun;
but the traveller, his mind aflame
with the fire of separation
from his sweetheart, dearly loved,
does not even think of the heat. (Haksar)[11]

---

8 Chandra Rajan, *Kālidāsa: The Loom of Time: A Selection of His Plays and Poems* (New Delhi: Penguin Books, 1989), p. 106.
9 Martha Ann Selby, *The Circle of Six Seasons: A Selection from Old Tamil, Prākrit and Sanskrit Poetry* (New Delhi: Penguin Books, 2003), p. 22.
10 Rajendra Tandon, *Kalidasa: Ritusamharam: The Garland of Seasons* (New Delhi: Rupa & Co, 2008), p. 71.
11 A. N. D. Haksar, *Kalidasa: Ritusamharam: A Gathering of Seasons* (New

Linguistic and Interpretive Translation

Even in the absence of formal constraints, some words of the Sanskrit text have been left untranslated in each of the above versions, while other words with no counterparts in the original have been introduced. Evidently it is not only exigencies of meter and rhyme that drive translators to take liberties with the literal meaning of the text. All such discrepancies are defects from the point of view of "linguistic translation," whose aim is a one-to-one mapping of linguistic elements from the source onto the target language (sometimes called "transcoding"). The "faithfulness" of translations is often evaluated according to the standards of this model. But its adequacy for understanding what translation is and how it works has been questioned.

"Interpretive translation" offers an alternative. Developed initially through observation of oral interpreting, this theory illuminates equally the process of literary translation. It is especially well suited for dealing with the intractable problems of translating poetry. The most distinctive feature of the interpretive model is the stage of "deverbalization" it posits between the comprehension of an utterance in one language and its reformulation in another. Marianne Lederer explains:

> Consecutive interpreters who succeed in retaining each nuance of sense before spontaneously re-expressing the whole discourse in their own language put into practice a very general aptitude which consists of retaining what has been understood whilst the words themselves disappear.
>
> Deverbalization may well be less obvious in translation than in consecutive interpreting but it is just as present. For interpreters and translators both, 'understanding' is arriving at a mental representation.[12]

Delhi: Penguin Books, 2018).
12 Marianne Lederer, *Translation: The Interpretive Model*, trans. Ninon Larché

A translation, then, directly expresses a mental representation and only indirectly the words from which that representation was constructed. To return to our example from *The Seasons*, the interpretive model helps to clarify how my translation came to depart as much as it does from the wording of the original, whose imagery, structure and feeling it nevertheless reproduces with what I believe to be a reasonable degree of fidelity. The interpretive theory also provides a basis for deciding whether or how much such verbal differences affect a translation's value.

Although I translated *The Seasons* before I had heard of deverbalization, the interpretive theory gives an accurate account of the method I followed. After internalizing a *śloka* through repeated readings, usually I composed the translation without looking again at the book. With the memory of the Sanskrit words still reverberating in my mind, my focus would shift to expressing in English the image they evoked. In this stanza, I was struck by the parallel phrasing of Kalidasa's second and fourth lines, which describe the fiery heat of the sun beating down on the earth (*sūrya-ātapa-tāpitā*, "sun-blaze-heated") and the fire of longing that consumes the hearts of those far from their loved ones (*viyoga-anala-dagdha*, "separation-fire-burned"). These sources of physical and emotional torment merged in my mental image to become the "two fires" of my first couplet:

> Blind with the dust that swirls across his way,
> The traveller endures two fires by day. . . .

Just as two Sanskrit words for fiery heat (*ātapa* and *anala*) are combined in these "two fires," so two words for heating or burning and the suffering they inflict (*tāpita* and *dagdha*) are replaced in my second couplet by the single word "afflicted." Moreover, the scorching effect of the sun's heat is transferred from the earth (*mahī*) to the body of the traveller making his way across it:

(New York: Routledge, 2014), p. 13.

His flesh afflicted by the sun above,
His heart by separation from his love.

Such liberties put this translation near the free end of the spectrum at whose other extreme is Kale's literalness. Perhaps my approach could best be described by the term "transcreation" favored by the late P. Lal, founder of Writers Workshop, at whose suggestion I first took up this project and who generously encouraged me in my approach. But in any case, according to the theory of interpretive translation, literary translators have a legitimate freedom of "spontaneous expression in the target language," so long as it is exercised to "faithfully recreate the global effect of the text on the reader."[13]

Mimetic and Analogical Form

A significant part of the effect of a poem, yet the part that can least be recreated in translation, is produced by its sound and form. One cannot read Sanskrit poetry without being impressed by the scrupulous attention the poets paid to the metrical molds into which they poured their inspiration. In the Indian literary tradition, the use of a variety of complex meters goes back to the Veda, reaching its height in the classical period. In ancient times, when Speech (*Vāk*) was a goddess, these rhythms were thought to be connected with the cosmic order. A remnant of this attitude survives even in the secular poetry of Kalidasa. It is perhaps not too far-fetched to find in the recurrent rhythmic patterns of his poem on the seasons a reflection of the regularity with which the seasons themselves recur in the cycles of time.

Since the metrical form of his works was clearly important to Kalidasa, it would seem appropriate for a translator of his poetry to consider the option of a metrical translation. As James Holmes observes, "there is an

---

13 Ibid., p. 84.

extremely close relationship between the kind of verse form a translator chooses and the kind of total effect his translation achieves."[14] When I set out to translate *The Seasons*, I had no preconceived ideas about what form it would take, metrical or otherwise. But a four-line stanza in a regular meter or meters soon emerged as the most promising way to convey something of the shapeliness and rhythmic dynamism of Kalidasa's *ślokas*.

This could only be done by drawing on the formal and metrical resources proper to the English language. To reproduce in English the intricate sequences of long and short syllables that constitute Sanskrit meters is much less possible than to imitate even the similarly quantitative meters of Greek and Latin. Holmes has coined the term "mimetic form" for this kind of imitation, as when Homer is translated in dactylic hexameters or Dante in terza rima.[15] Isolated attempts to copy Sanskrit meters in English have occasionally been made for the purpose of illustration.[16] However, it is doubtful whether any such exercise could be sustained for long or would result in a readable translation producing an effect at all like that of the original.

The only way to reflect the structure and rhythmic impetus of Kalidasa's stanzas, therefore, is through what Holmes calls "analogical form." Translators following this route, he explains, have "looked beyond the original poem itself to the function of its form within its poetic tradition, then sought a form that filled a parallel function within the poetic tradition of the target language."[17] In English, with its relatively limited repertoire

---

14 James S. Holmes, "Forms of Verse Translation and the Translation of Verse Form," in Holmes, ed., *The Nature of Translation: Essays on the Theory and Practice of Literary Translation* (The Hague: Mouton and Co., 1970), p. 101.

15 Ibid., p. 95.

16 For example, see John Brough, *Poems from the Sanskrit* (New York: Penguin Books, 1968), pp. 43–44.

17 Holmes, "Forms of Verse Translation and the Translation of Verse Form," pp. 95–96.

of metrical options, the choice can first be narrowed down to the flexible iambic meters which can most easily be modulated to create a variety of rhythmic moods and effects. Among these, the five-foot line – the iambic pentameter, which for centuries has been used for most English poetry even remotely comparable to Kalidasa's in style or scope – immediately recommends itself.

But at this point a problem arises. Four principal meters occur in *Ṛtusaṃhāra*. Those with eleven or twelve syllables in a *pāda* generally lend themselves well enough to translation in the iambic pentameter, whose length of only ten syllables is a safeguard against padding. Kalidasa employs one or other of these shorter meters (usually the eleven-syllable *upajāti* or twelve-syllable *vaṃśastha*) for the first part of almost every season, creating a metrical variation from one canto to the next that can be reflected in English by using different rhyme schemes. Toward the end of each season, however, he changes meters. Normally he switches from an eleven- or twelve-syllable to a fourteen- or fifteen-syllable meter (*vasantatilakā* or *mālinī*). In "Autumn" the change is from fourteen syllables to fifteen.

If the quatrain form is kept as a way of representing the four-*pāda* structure of the *śloka*, ten syllables in a line tend to be not enough for translating the longer Sanskrit meters. When I came to these meters, therefore, I found it necessary to add another foot to each line. This means that in the later part of almost every canto, where Kalidasa switches to a longer meter, the meter of the translation also changes from iambic pentameter to the iambic hexameter or Alexandrine. The exception is "Autumn," which has been translated entirely in Alexandrines. There is also a single *śloka* in a nineteen-syllable meter (*śārdūlavikrīḍita*) at the very end of the Sanskrit text. This could not be squeezed into four lines in the translation and required special treatment.

Translating Sanskrit Meters

Meter is only a skeleton of the body of sound that is fleshed out in lines of actual poetry. The use of metrical forms in a translation, especially forms that do not closely resemble those of the original, is justified only if it communicates an aspect of the source that would otherwise be lost. In the last century or so, there has been a sharp decline in the appreciation of what metrical rhythm and rhyme contribute to poetry. Under such circumstances, translators may be excused for not wanting to complicate their task by struggling to give a sense of the formal features of classical works. In the present translation, I have departed in this respect from current practice because it seemed to me that the rhythmic *élan* of Kalidasa's poetry was too vital a characteristic to sacrifice for the more subdued movement of prose or even free verse.

The iambic pentameter quatrain – traditionally called the heroic or elegiac stanza – whether with the standard rhyme scheme (ABAB) or as a double couplet (AABB), provided an adaptable "analogical form" for *ślokas* in the shorter Sanskrit meters. The Alexandrine posed more of a challenge. This is a meter whose employment in English poetry has been largely confined to single lines in poems written mainly in other meters, as in the last line of a Spenserian stanza or the stanzas of Shelley's "To a Skylark." Judging it unsuited for more extensive or continuous use, Fraser states bluntly: "A whole poem written in Alexandrines would tire the ear."[18] Sri Aurobindo was asked by a correspondent about the reasons for the neglect of the Alexandrine in English. Acknowledging that "no one has ever been able to make effective use of it as a staple metre," he offered this comment:

> The difficulty, I suppose, is its normal tendency to fall into two monotonously equal halves while the possible variations on that monotony seem to stumble often into awkward inequalities. . . .

---

18 G. S. Fraser, *Metre, Rhyme and Free Verse* (New York: Routledge, 2018).

All this, however, may be simply because the secret of the right handling has not been found.[19]

In practice, I have found this relatively unexplored meter to have untapped potential as a vehicle for translating Kalidasa's poetry. Specifically, I have used it for passages in the fourteen- and fifteen-syllable meters called *vasantatilakā* and *mālinī*. These are defined by the following quite different sequences of long and short syllables:

– – ⏑ – ⏑ ⏑ ⏑ – ⏑ ⏑ – ⏑ – – (*vasantatilakā*)

⏑ ⏑ ⏑ ⏑ ⏑ ⏑ – – – ⏑ – – ⏑ – – (*mālinī*)

An example of the second of these meters is the following *śloka* in "Summer" describing the spread of a forest fire:

ज्वलति पवनवृद्धः पर्वतानां दरीषु
स्फुटति पटुनिनादैः शुष्कवंशस्थलीषु ।
प्रसरति तृणमध्ये लब्धवृद्धिः क्षणेन
ग्लपयति मृगवर्गं प्रान्तलग्नो दवाग्निः ॥

jvalati pavana-vṛddhaḥ parvatānāṁ darīṣu
sphuṭati paṭu-ninādaiḥ śuṣka-vaṁśa-sthalīṣu,
prasarati tṛṇa-madhye labdha-vṛddhiḥ kṣaṇena
glapayati mṛga-vargaṁ prānta-lagno davāgniḥ.

This is translated literally by Kale: "The conflagration, starting on the skirts (of woodland), torments all beasts; increasing with the wind it burns in the mountain valleys; it breaks forth with sharp noises in places (abounding) with dry bamboos; growing strong in a moment it spreads in the grass."[20] In translating this *śloka*, I had to omit the animals who appear briefly near the end (and reappear two stanzas later), focusing

---

19 Sri Aurobindo, *Letters on Poetry and Art* (Pondicherry: Sri Aurobindo Ashram, 2004), p. 131–32.
20 Kale, *The Ṛtusaṁhāra of Kālidāsa*, p. 81.

on the fire's irresistible momentum as it races across the countryside consuming everything in its path:

> Kindled in lowland thickets, strong winds lead it higher
> Until the distant hills and valleys are afire.
> Resonantly it crackles in the dry bamboo,
> Then sweeps with huge destruction through the grasses, too.

Rhythmically, *mālinī* with its opening series of six short syllables is an ideal meter for depicting rapid movement. An echo of this rhythm has, I believe, found its way into the translation, especially in the third line, "Resonantly it crackles in the dry bamboo," where a run of short syllables in the first half of the line produces an effect not unlike that of the Sanskrit.

To illustrate the *vasantatilakā*, let us take a picture of gentler movement from a mellower season, "Autumn":

आकम्पयन्फलभरानतशालिजाला-
न्यानर्तयंस्तरुवरान्कुसुमावनम्रान् ।
उत्फुल्लपङ्कजवनां नलिनीं विधुन्व-
न्यूनां मनश्चलयति प्रसभं नभस्वान् ॥

*ākampayan phala-bharānata-śāli-jālāny
ānartayaṁs taru-varān kusumāvanamrān,
utphulla-paṅkaja-vanāṁ nalinīṁ vidhunvan
yūnāṁ manaś calayati prasabhaṁ nabhasvān.*

Kale's literal translation reads: "The breeze is forcibly unsettling the minds of young men, as it is shaking the rows of *śāli* corn bent with a heavy crop, is tossing fine trees hanging down with flowers, (and) is waving the lotus-plant with a number of lotuses blooming on it."[21] Here is my rendering:

---

21 Ibid., p. 89. 162–63

> Ripe, burdened stalks are dancing in the paddy field
> While, wrestling with the wind, the tree-tops toss and yield;
> A vivid wave of petals is the lotus pond –
> When Nature is astir, what heart will not respond?

Here the first phrase, "Ripe, burdened stalks," duplicates the metrical pattern (– – ⌣ –) with which the *vasantatilakā* meter begins, in contrast to the swiftness of the opening sequence of short syllables in the *mālinī*. I have made no attempt, however, to introduce such reminiscences of the original rhythm as a systematic part of the technique of the translation. In handling the Alexandrine, as these examples show, I have tried to avoid the "monotonously equal halves" that Sri Aurobindo warned against by often delaying slightly the pause which tends to occur in the middle of each line. Here, for instance, it comes after "dancing" and "petals" in the first and third lines, dividing these lines into units of seven and five syllables instead of six and six. Judiciously done, I believe that varying the position of the caesura in this way need not result in the "awkward inequalities" which are this meter's opposite pitfall.

The Rationale of This Translation

Whatever the length of the lines, basically the same means must be used to heighten ordinary English speech rhythms if there is to be any kind of replication of the musical properties of Sanskrit poetry. Accentual verse in English combines regularity in its underlying metrical framework with flexibility in its actual rhythms to achieve the range of expressive power that is potentially at a poet's or translator's disposal. Sri Aurobindo explains how this works:

> What we really have is a system of recurrent strokes or beats intervening at a fixed place in each foot, while the syllables which

are not hammered into prominent place by this kind of stroke or beat fill the interspaces. A regular metrical base is thus supplied, but the rhythm can be varied or modulated by departures from the base – from it but always upon it; for these departures, variations or modulations, relieve its regularity which might otherwise become monotonous, but do not replace or frustrate the essential rhythm.[22]

Sanskrit prosody follows another principle altogether. Based on syllabic length rather than accent, the patterns defining its typical meters have enough internal variety that they can be repeated unchanged up to a certain point without monotony. English prosody, on the other hand, not only permits but practically requires the use of substitutions such as that of a trochee (– ⏑), spondee (– –), pyrrhic (⏑ ⏑) or anapaest (⏑ ⏑ –) for an iamb (⏑ –). It is only by a sensitive resort to such departures from the metrical base that so mechanical a formula as that of the iambic pentameter (⏑ – | ⏑ – | ⏑ – | ⏑ – | ⏑ –) can be turned into a launching pad for endless expressive variations.

These resources of the English metrical tradition have been exploited to the full in this translation. Its purpose has been to recreate to some extent, though by different means than those available in Sanskrit, what I perceive as vital qualities of the rhythmic atmosphere of the original. This could not be done without taking advantage of the disciplined freedom of creative expression recognized in the interpretive theory as the literary translator's prerogative. Whether the experiment has been fruitful or not is, in the end, for the readers to decide.

In *The Wonder That Was India*, A. L. Basham felt compelled to acknowledge a discouraging fact for enthusiasts of Indian culture: "On the whole classical Sanskrit literature has not been well received in the West.

---

22 Sri Aurobindo, *The Future Poetry with On Quantitative Metre* (Pondicherry: Sri Aurobindo Ashram, 1997), p. 326.

Though the works of Kālidāsa delighted Goethe, the literature taken as a whole has been called artificial, over-ornate, lacking in true feeling."[23] This was written in the 1950s by one who was himself an admirer of ancient Indian civilization. The widespread lack of appreciation of which he spoke, insofar as it persists, is largely due to a misunderstanding which perhaps only translators are in a position to remedy.

The present version of *The Seasons* is meant to contribute to such an effort through the exploration of a distinctive approach whose rationale I have explained in some detail. This adventure has been the result of drinking deeply of the *rasa* of Kalidasa's poetry and savoring equally the *rasa* of life which is its source. The translation will succeed in its aim if it transmits a taste of this exhilarating experience to even a few receptive readers.

---

23 A. L. Basham, *The Wonder That Was India: A Survey of the Culture of the Indian Sub-Continent before the Coming of the Muslims* (New York: Grove Press, 1959).

Canto 1
Summer

গ্রীষ্ম—ঋতুসংহার পৃঃ ১ম

प्रचण्डसूर्यः स्पृहणीयचन्द्रमाः
सदावगाहक्षतवारिसञ्चयः ।
दिनान्तरम्योऽभ्युपशान्तमन्मथो
निदाघकालोऽयमुपागतः प्रिये ॥ १ ॥

* * *

নিদাঘের কাল সমাগত প্রিয়া
ভাস্কর-কর প্রচণ্ড অতি
ইন্দু-কিরণ-সুধা বাঞ্ছিত
অতি স্নানে বারি নাহি এক রতি
দিবা অবসনে রম্য সকলি,
শান্ত চিত্ত, বাসনা বিহীন ;
যৌবন-তাপ খর নাহি আর
ক্লান্তির ভরে কাটিতেছে দিন ! ১

* * *

Now the sun's fury grows, the moon's delight;
Now all day long the splashing pools invite.
Evenings are blissful and desire, my dear,
Languishes – oh, the summertime is here! (1)

निशाः शशाङ्कक्षतनीलरजयः
　　क्वचिद् विचित्रं जलयन्त्रमन्दिरम्।
मणिप्रकाराः सरसं च चन्दनं
　　शुचौ प्रिये यान्ति जनस्य सेव्यताम् ॥ २॥

* * *

শশাঙ্ক আসি তিমিরে হরিলে
দেখা দিলে বধূ, স্নিগ্ধ রাতি,
বিচিত্র জল-যন্ত্র-ঘরেতে
রস-চন্দন, হিম-মণি ভাতি
অতি প্রিয় এই গ্রীষ্মের দিনে
উপভোগ তারি চায় সদা মন
ভাগ্য প্রবল, বাসনা পূরিত
ভাবিয়া সকলে করে তা গ্রহণ !　২

* * *

Nights when the moonlight drives the dark away,
Pavilions on the lake where fountains play,
Moist sandal cream and gems that cool the skin:
Such things, my love, one now takes pleasure in. (2)

সুবাসিতং হর্ম্যতলং মনোহরং
   প্রিয়ামুখোচ্ছ্বাসবিকম্পিতং মধু।
সুতন্ত্রিগীতং মদনস্য দীপনং
   শুচৌ নিশীথেঽনুভবন্তি কামিনঃ ॥ ৩॥

* * *

বিলাস-লালসে মগন জনায়
হর্ম্য পলরে সুবাসে ভরিয়া
প্রিয়ার বদন উচ্ছাস কাঁপন
মধু-সুধা লয়ে বীণাটি ধরিয়া,
তন্ত্রী-গীতির মরমের গানে
গাহি, বাসনার করিছে উদয় ;
রস অনুভব সুগভীর লভি
নিদাঘ-নিশীথে সুখ ভরি রয় !   ৩

* * *

The perfumes of the terrace, where one sips
Wine rippling with the breath from honeyed lips,
While music raises rapture to its height –
Sweet the enjoyments of a summer night! (3)

नितम्बबिम्बैः सदुकूलमेखलैः
    स्तनैः सहाराभरणैः सचन्दनैः ।
शिरोरुहैः स्नानकषायवासितैः
    स्त्रियो निदाघं शमयन्ति कामिनाम् ॥ ४॥

* * *

কোমল সূক্ষ্ম বসন, মেখলা
গুরু-নিতম্বে সুশোভিত রহি
স্রক্-চন্দন বক্ষের ভারে
স্নানেতে সুরভি সুগন্ধ বহি,
আনন্দে কাল কাটায় ললনা
অলকেরে করি পরম শোভন ;
নিদাঘের তাপে শান্তি আনিয়া
কামিনীরা করে কামনা পূরণ ! ৪

* * *

With silk-clad, girdled hips and strings of pearls
Embellishing their bosoms, gracious girls,
Hair fragrant from the bath, employ their arts
To soothe the burning in their lovers' hearts. (4)

नितान्तलाक्षारसरागरञ्जितैर्नि
    म्बिनीनां चरणैः सनूपुरैः ।
पदे पदे हंसरुतानकारिभिर्ज
    नस्य चित्तं क्रियते समन्मथम् ॥ ५॥

* * *

নিতান্ত লাল লাক্ষায় পদ
    রাঙায়ে নূপুর, হাঁসে অনুকারী,
নিক্কণি চলি যায় যে রমণী
    বাসনা উদয় পদে পদে তারি !   ৫

* * *

The scarlet of their decorated feet,
Their languid walk while anklet bells repeat
A silver mimicry of cackling geese
At every step, deprive the mind of peace. (5)

पयोधराश्चन्दनपङ्कचर्चितास्तु
    षारगौरार्पितहारशेखराः ।
नितम्बदेशाश्च सहेममेखलाः
    प्रकुर्वते कस्य मनो न सोत्सुकम् ॥ ६॥

* * *

চন্দন-রসে চর্চ্চিত শ্বেত
বক্ষে, হিমানী-ধবলিত হারে,
বিম্বাধরার শোভে নিতম্বে
কনক-মেখলা, নেহারিয়া তারে
নীরস-কঠিন আছে কেবা হেন
এহেন সরস ভাব দেখি হায় !
বল কে না রহে ব্যাকুলতা ভরে
লভিতে কাহার মন নাহি চায় ? ৬

* * *

The scent of sandal rubbed into their breasts,
The snow-white necklace that between them rests,
The hips on which a golden girdle swings –
Whose senses are not ravished by these things? (6)

समुद्रतस्वेदचिताङ्गसंधयो
विमुच्य वासांसि गुरूणि सांप्रतम् ।
स्तनेषु तन्वंशुकमुन्नतस्तना
निवेशयन्ति प्रमदाः सयौवनाः ॥ ७॥

* * *

তনু-সন্ধিতে ভরি যায় স্বেদ,
গুরু-বসনেরে এবে তুলে রাখি
বক্ষে সূক্ষ্ম বসন ধরিয়া
প্রমদা তরুণী নিতেছে ঢাকি ! ৭

* * *

Relieving now of heavier attire
Young limbs whose joints and crevices perspire,
Across their swelling chests they only drape
Sheer fabrics that reveal the wearer's shape. (7)

৪

তবু শাজির তারি দাস রূপ,
গুরু-আসনে এবে তুলে রাখি
রক্ত মুখর অধর দাপিয়া
প্রমদা তরুণী- নিলাজ ঢাকি ! ৭৫

দোদুল-বারি ব্রজের বধূবর,
বুক ঢাকা হার, মালার ভূষণ,
বীণ-কানের সাথ সঙ্গীতে
নাচিয়া জাগায় ঊষিন রমন ! ৮

নিশি-ভাঙ্গিয়া চিত- চঞ্চিতে
মুখ-চুমুয় নাগরিকা সার,
বেদনি বাণ গেহ তঁহুতে
রাতি অবসান ব্রহ্মরাত মার
কাজল- কাপুয়ে রহি মন কান
তিতা সাটি অমনি পলায়
অর্দ্ধেক মুখী হরি ঢাঁখু ঘুরা
সাথ সাথ তার রজনী বিদায়! ১

सचन्दनाम्बुव्यजनोद्भवानिलैः
    सहारयष्टिस्तनमण्डलार्पणैः ।
सवल्लकीकाकलिगीतनिस्वनैर्
    विबोध्यते सुप्त इवाद्य मन्मथः ॥ ८ ॥

* * *

চন্দন-বারি ব্যজনের ছিটা,
বুকে ঢাকা হার, মালার ভূষণ,
বীণা-বাদনের সাথে সঙ্গীতে
লভিয়া জাগিয়া উঠিল মদন ! ৮

* * *

Fans stirring up an aromatic breeze,
Singing a veena's twang accompanies,
And nudging breasts fine threads of pearls adorn
Awake the love-god on a summer morn. (8)

সিতেষু হর্ম্যেষু নিশাসু যোষিতাং
সুখপ্রসুপ্তানি মুখানি চন্দ্রমাঃ ।
বিলোক্য নূনং ভৃশমুৎসুকশ্চিরং
নিশাক্ষয়ে যাতি হ্রিয়েব পাণ্ডুতাম্ ॥ ৯ ॥

* * *

নিশি-চন্দ্রিমা সিত সৌধেতে
সুখ-প্রসুপ্ত নাগরিকা সবে,
নেহারি বদন ম'হা উৎসুকে
রাতি অবসানে তরাসেতে যাবে
লাজে পাণ্ডু সে রহি ক্ষণকাল
বিগত কান্তি অমনি পলায়
অধরের সুধা হরি ল'য়ে ত্বরা
সাথে সাথে তার রজনী বিদায় ! ৯

* * *

Women asleep in mansions glimmering white
Betray their faces to the wistful sight
Of the long-gazing moon, whose look turns wan
As if with guilt at the approach of dawn. (9)

असह्यवातोद्धतरेणुमण्डला
प्रचण्डसूर्यातपतापिता मही ।
न शक्यते द्रष्टमपि प्रवासिभिः
प्रियावियोगानलदग्धमानसैः ॥ १० ॥

* * *

অসহ্য বায়ু উদ্ধৃত ধূলি
দগ্ধ-তপ্ত ভাস্করে সহী ;
প্রিয়া-বিরহীর সন্তাপ মনে
আসে তার কাছে গুরুভার বহি ! ১০

* * *

Blind with the dust that swirls across his way,
The traveller endures two fires by day,
His flesh afflicted by the sun above,
His heart by separation from his love. (10)

मृगाः प्रचण्डातपतापिता भृशं
    तृषा महत्या परिशुष्कतालवः ।
वनान्तरे तोयमिति प्रधाविता
    निरीक्ष्य भिन्नाञ्जनसंनिभं नभः ॥ ११ ॥

* * *

প্রবল তাপেতে তাপিত হরিণী
তালুকা শুষ্ক, তৃষার কারণ,
দলিত আঁজন অধিক চিকন
গগনের শোভা, তুলিয়া নয়ন
মরীচিকা হেরি, জল আশে ফিরি,
বন-বনান্তে সবেগেতে ধায় ;
মিটেনা তিয়াষা তারি সন্ধানে
ব্যর্থ কোথাও বারি নাহি পায় ! ১১

* * *

Antelopes overheated by the sun,
Their palates parched with thirst, are seen to run
In quest of a mirage, for they mistake
The blue on the horizon for a lake. (11)

সবিভ্রমৈঃ সস্মিতজিহ্মবীক্ষিতৈর্
 বিলাসবত্যো মনসি প্রবাসিনাম্ ।
অনঙ্গসংদীপনমাশু কুর্বতে
 যথা প্রদোষাঃ শশিচারুভূষণাঃ ॥ ১২॥

* * *

শশি-চারু সাজে প্রদোষের কালে
আনন্দে সুখে প্রবাসীর মনে
যেভাবে জাগে গো, বিলাসবতীর
হাসি-সংশয় কুটিল নয়নে,
মনেরে ভুলায়ে তাহাদেরে তারা
মধুরসে ভরি জর জরি তোলে ;
এমনি চাতুরী নাগরীরা ধরি
নিদাঘ কালের সন্তাপে ভোলে ! ১২

* * *

Coquettish maidens, with their laughing eyes
And movements that allure and tantalize,
Like moonbeams on a starry eve impart
Refreshment to the wayfarer's worn heart. (12)

রবের্ময়ূখৈরভিতাপিতো ভৃশং
  বিদহ্যমানঃ পথি তপ্তপাংসুভিঃ ।
অবাঙ্খো জিহ্মগতিঃ শ্বসন্মুহুঃ
  ফণী ময়ূরস্য তলে নিষীদতি ॥ ১৩ ॥

* * *

প্রভাকর-কর-কিরণ-ময়ূখে
ভুজঙ্গ তাপে তাপিত ধূলায়
দঘধি দীঘল ঘন ঘন শ্বাসে
বিসর্পি ধীরে লুকাইতে চায় ;
অধোমুখে ধায় নিদাঘের ভারে
ময়ূর যেথায় বিরাজিয়া থাকে,
তারি তলদেশে বিরামের লাগি
কোনোমতে বহি নিজেরে সে রাখে ! ১৩

* * *

With drooping head, a breathless serpent winds
Across the burning sand until it finds
A refuge from the overwhelming heat
Among the shadows at a peacock's feet. (13)

তৃষা মহত্যা হতবিক্রমোদ্যমঃ
শ্বসন্মুহুর্দূরবিদারিতাননঃ ।
ন হন্ত্যদূরেঽপি গজান্মৃগেশ্বরো
বিলোলজিহ্বশ্চলিতাগ্রকেসরঃ ॥ ১৪ ॥

* * *

মহতী তৃষাতে হত-বিক্রম
বিলোল-জিহ্বা শ্বাস ঘন পড়ে,
কেশরীরা কেশ চূড়া কাঁপাইয়া
করীরে হেরিয়া বিনাশ না করে ! ১৪

* * *

Lions with lolling tongues, huge yawning jaws
And wind-stirred manes lift not their dreadful paws
Against the elephants, whom they permit
To pass where panting mightily they sit. (14)

विशुष्ककण्ठोद्वतशीकराम्भसो
गभस्तिभिर्भानुमतोऽभितापिताः ।
प्रवृद्धतृष्णोपहता जलार्थिनो
न दन्तिनः केसरिणोऽपि बिभ्यति ॥ १५॥

* * *

মাতঙ্গ, রবি তাপেতে [কাহিল !],
তৃষায় কণ্ঠ শুষ্ক কারণ,
ভয় নাহি পায় সিংহে নেহারি
সলিল ধারায় করে আহরণ ! ১৫

* * *

Assaulted by the sun's relentless rays,
An elephant with trunk uplifted sprays
Some drops down his dry throat, nor does he heed
The king of beasts, so desperate his need. (15)

গ্রীষ্মখতু

মলয়, রবি আলোক ....,
হুতাশ করে শুষ্ক কাণ্ঠ;
ভয় নাই কার মিলিবে নেহারি
সলিল দেবার করে আহ্বান! ১৫

অশুচি- গ্লানি ক্লিষ্ট ভূধর—
কিরাত কুটির দেহমন ভার;
কলঙ্কী সে সুখ কলাপচন্দ্র
নিরাশাদীপ্ত রাখি, হারাই না বিবেক!২১

রুচি-কর-লোক-সপর্শ বরণ—
ভয়না- খুশারে লাগিল ভুবন—
এখানা অধিক মাতায়ার মান—
ঘন কাহিনী শুভ্র কল্যাণ—
দেখে মন, দীপ হেরিবাদ সান্ত্র
দুঃখিনী সহে হৃদয়ালিত দুঃ;
ও উঠায়িতে ওর কমল সরূর্ত—
রা কার ধ্যান কপড় সাধ্য ভূমি হয়!২৭

हुताग्निकल्पैः सवितुर्गभस्तिभिः
    कलापिनः क्लान्तशरीरचेतसः ।
न भोगिनं घ्नन्ति समीपवर्तिनं
    कलापचक्रेषु निवेशिताननम् ॥ १६ ॥

* * *

আহুতি-অগ্নি সদৃশ সূর্য্য
কিরণে ক্লান্তি দেহ মনে ভ'রে ;
কলাপী সে মুখ কলাপচক্রে
নিবেশিয়া রাখি, অহিরে না ধরে ! ১৬

* * *

Beams flaming down from heaven, like the fire
That flares up in the sacrifice, so tire
The peacock that his natural instincts fail
To make him strike the snake beneath his tail. (16)

সভদ্রমুস্তং পরিশুষ্ককর্দমং
সরঃ খনন্রায়তপোত্রমণ্ডলৈঃ ।
রবের্ময়ূখৈরভিতাপিতো ভৃশং
বরাহযূথো বিশতীব ভূতলম্ ॥ ১৭ ॥

* * *

রবি-কর-তাপে তাপিত বরাহ
ভাদ্লা-মুথারে পাইবারে চায়
আয়ত অধরে সরোবর মাঝে
খনন করিছে শুষ্ক কাদায়
দেখে মনে হয়, নাশিবারে তাপ
ভূমির গর্ভে প্রবেশিতে ত্বরা ;
জুড়াইতে তার বাসনা সদাই
করে যায় কাজ গায়ে ধূলি ভরা ! ১৭

* * *

A lake stood where a herd of feral pigs
Through dying weeds and drying mud now digs
With long snouts for the trickles that exude
From pits whence only their hind ends protrude. (17)

विवस्वता तीक्ष्णतरांशुमालिना
	सपङ्कतोयात्सरसोऽभितापितः ।
उत्प्लुत्य भेकस्तृषितस्य भोगिनः
	फणातपत्रस्य तले निषीदति ॥ १८ ॥

* * *

পঙ্কিল নীর উৎপ্লুত ভেক
তৃষিত সাপের ফণার ছাতায়,
প্রচণ্ড তাপে লয় আশ্রয়,
ভয় নাহি পায় পায় জীবন জুড়ায় ! ১৮

* * *

The pond diminished to a muddy bog
Beneath the sun's ferocious siege, a frog
Hops from its puddle, for the shade is good
Under the shelter of a cobra's hood. (18)

समुद्रताशेषमृणालजालकं
विपन्नमीनं द्रुतभीतसारसं
परस्परोत्पीडनसंहतैर्गजैः
कृतं सरः सान्द्रविमर्दकर्दमम् ॥ १९ ॥

* * *

পরস্পরের পীড়নেতে করী
উদ্ধৃত করি মৃণালের জাল
কর্দ্দমে ভরি সরোবর জলে
বিপন্ন মীন, সারসের পাল -
ভীত সচকিত হয় তারা সবে,
পড়ে সোরগোল, করে পলায়ন ;
নিদাঘের কালে রীতি এই সখি !
এমনি যে হয় বিপদ তখন ! ১৯

* * *

Uprooted lotuses strewn all about,
Fish perishing, flamingoes put to rout,
A jostling crowd of elephants can make
A sea of mire where once there was a lake. (19)

রবিপ্রভোদ্দিপ্তশিরোমণিভো
বিলোলজিহ্বাদ্বয়লীঢমারুতঃ।
বিষাগ্নিসূর্যাতপতাপিতঃ ফণী
ন হন্তি মণ্ডুককুলং তৃষাকুলঃ ॥ ২০॥

* * *

বিষ দাবানল, আতপে তাপিত
ভুজঙ্গ তৃষায় আকুলি বিকুলি
বিলোল জিহ্বা বায়ুর লেহনে
হিংসা তাহারা গিয়াছে যে ভুলি !
আদিত্যরাগে শিরোমণি বিভা,
প্রভা বিস্তারি, মণ্ডূকে হেরি
বিনাশ না করে গ্রীষ্মের দিনে
খাদ্য, খাদক আনন্দে ঘেরি ! ২০

* * *

Its jewelled hood more brilliant in the glare,
Its forked tongue licking at the sultry air,
A snake oppressed by heat and by its own
Secreted venom leaves the frogs alone. (20)

सफेनलालावृतवक्त्रसंपुटं
विनिःसृतालोहितजह्वमुन्मुखम् ।
तृषाकुलं निःसृतमद्रिगह्वराद्
अवेक्षमाणं महिषीकुलं जलम् ॥ २१ ॥

* * *

লেলিহান লাল জিভে ফেনা ঝরে
মহিষেরা সবে তৃষ্ণায় ভরি,
গিরি গুহা হ'তে বাহিরিয়া আসি
চঞ্চলি ধায় মুখ উঁচা করি ! ২১

* * *

With upturned muzzles from which dangle pink
And foam-bespeckled tongues, in search of drink
Wild buffaloes, compelled by thirst to brave
The sun's blaze, issue from a mountain cave. (21)

पटुतरदवदाहोच्छुष्कसस्यप्ररोहाः
परुषपवनवेगोत्क्षिप्तसंशुष्कपर्णाः ।
दिनकरपरितापक्षीणतोयाः समन्ताद्
विदधति भयमुच्चैर्वीक्ष्यमाणा वनान्ताः ॥ २२॥

* * *

অতীব প্রবল দাব-দাহ তরে
শষ্যাঙ্কুর বিদগ্ধ সবি,
দিনকর তাপে শুষ্ক তটিণী
খর-কিরণের পরশনে রবি
ঝটিকা বাত্যা বেগেতে ছড়ায়ে,
শুকানো পর্ণ, বনানীর তলে ;
প্রাপ্ত হইতে ভয় হয় হেরি
সেই কালে সখি, নিদাঘ যে বলে ! ২২

* * *

Bleak, desiccated fields where forest fires have passed,
Parched leaves whirled from the branches by the wind's sharp blast,
Streams shrunken to a trickle by the scorching sun –
The spectacle of the woodlands is a dismal one. (22)

श्वसिति विहगवर्गःशीर्णपर्णद्रुमस्थः
कपिकुलमुपयाति क्लान्तमद्रेर्निकुञ्जम् ।
भ्रमति गवययूथः सर्वतस्तोयमिच्छञ्
शरभकुलमजिह्मं प्रोद्धरत्यम्बु कूपात् ॥ २३॥

* * *

শীর্ণ পত্র গাছে বসে পাখী
বসিছে সেথায় জীবনেরে ধরি ;
ক্লান্ত কপিরা, গিরি-নিকুঞ্জে
যায় চলি দূরে শ্রান্তিতে ভরি !
গাভীরা সলিল খুঁজিয়া ফিরিছে
গোঠেমাঠে সদা বন-প্রান্তরে,
শরভেরা সব সরল ভাবেতে
কূপ হ'তে জল আহরিছে ধরে ! ২৩

* * *

Birds in the barren tree-tops pant with drooping bills;
The monkeys have retreated high into the hills;
Wild oxen roam in thirst and elephant cubs try
To stretch their trunks for water in a well gone dry. (23)

विकचनवकुसुम्भस्वच्छसिन्दूरभासा
प्रबलपवनवेगोद्धतवेगेन तूर्णम् ।
तरुविटपलताग्रालिङ्गनव्याकुलेन
दिशि दिशि परिदग्धा भूमयः पावकेन ॥ २४ ॥

* * *

তীব্র পবন বেগ সম্ভূত
হুতাশন নব-কুসুম্ভ ফুলে
সচ্ছ সিঁদুর আভা বিস্তারি,
তট-বিটপের লতাগ্রে দুলে
দিশি দিশি পরিদগ্ধিয়া ফেরে
ভূভাগ পাবক বিনাশিয়া ছোটে ;
অরণ্যের মাঝে রুদ্র সে রূপ
রক্তিম আভা উজ্জ্বলি ওঠে ! ২৪

* * *

Crimson like full-blown safflower or vermilion red,
Whipped to a rage by sudden gusts and quickly spread,
Clasping the twigs and creepers in a hot embrace,
To every side the legions of the wildfire race. (24)

ज्वलति पवनवृद्धः पर्वतानां दरीषु
स्फुटति पटुनिनादः शुष्कवंशस्थलीषु ।
प्रसरति तृणमध्ये लब्धवृद्धिः क्षणेन
ग्लपयति मृगवर्गं प्रान्तलग्नो दवाग्निः ॥ २५॥

* * *

বায়ু দাবাগ্নি বর্দ্ধিত কার
গিরি কন্দরে প্রজ্জ্বলি থাকে
স্ফুটিত গভীর নিনাদে শুষ্ক
বংশস্থলীরে ধ্বংসীয়া তাকে
বৃদ্ধি লভিয়া ধায় পুনরায়
বনভূমি শেষে তৃণের উপরে ;
ব্যাকুল মৃগেরা ভ্রমে চারিভিতে
নিকটে যখন দাবানল ধরে ! ২৫

* * *

Kindled in lowland thickets, strong winds lead it higher
Until the distant hills and valleys are afire.
Resonantly it crackles in the dry bamboo,
Then sweeps with huge destruction through the grasses, too. (25)

बहुतर इव जातः शाल्मलीनां वनेषु
स्फुरति कनकगौरः कोटरेषु द्रुमाणाम् ।
परिणतदलशाखानुत्पतन्भ्रांशुवृक्षान्
भ्रमति पवनधूतः सर्वतोऽग्निर्वनान्ते ॥ २६ ॥

* * *

শিমুলের বনে পশিয়া বহ্নি
বহুরূপ লয়ে জনম সে পায়,
লভিয়া গৌর-কনক-কান্তি
তরুর কোটরে প্রবেশিতে ধায় ;
পবনের বেগে দীপ্তি লভিয়া
উচ্চপাদপ, পরিণত শাখে,
ঊর্দ্ধে উঠিয়া সঞ্চারি চলি
বনপ্রান্তর অগ্নিতে ঢাকে । ২৬

* * *

Flames mingle with the flowers of the silk-cotton trees;
They lick the hollow trunks and flicker in the breeze.
Climbing the leafless branches in a blaze of gold,
They crown the dizzy tops, a splendor to behold. (26)

গজগবয়মৃগেন্দ্রা বহ্নিসংতপ্তদেহা
সুহৃদ ইব সমেতা দ্বন্দ্বভাবং বিহায়।
হুতবহপরিখেদাদাশু নির্গত্য কক্ষাদ্
বিপুলপুলিনদেশাং নিম্নগাং সংবিশন্তি ॥ ২৭॥

* * *

হুতাশন তাপে তপ্ত শরীর
গজ, গাভী, মৃগ-ইন্দ্রেরা সবে
দ্বন্দ্বের ভাব ছাড়ি দিয়া তারা
মিলিছে সুখেতে একসাথে যবে,
অপ্ত গিরির কন্দর ছাড়ি
বিপুল পুলিন তটভরা নদী
আশ্রয় তরে নামি দেয় পাড়ি
নিদাঘে সেথায় সুখ পায় যদি ! ২৭

* * *

Elephants, lions, herds of oxen congregate
Like refugees, forgetting mutual fear and hate.
Chased by the conflagration from their homes, they reach
The safety of a river's broad and sandy beach. (27)

कमलवनचिताम्बुः पाटलामोदरम्यः
        सुखसलिलनिषेकः सेव्यचन्द्रांशुहारः ।
व्रजतु तव निदाघः कामिनीभिः समेतो
        निशि सुललितगीते हर्म्यपृष्ठे सुखेन ॥ २८ ॥
इति ग्रीष्मवर्णनं नाम प्रथमः सर्गः ॥

* * *

কমল-কানন সলিলে ভরিয়া
জল-সেক লভি শরীর জুড়ায়,
পাটল কুসুমে সবাসিত রহি
ইন্দু কিরণে পুষ্প মালায় ;
সম্ভোগি সুখে সুললিত গীতি
সৌধে বসিয়া, নিদাঘের নিশি
কাটাও হে সখা, ভরি ল'য়ে প্রীতি
কামিনীর সাথে কামনায় মিশি ! ২৮
        গ্রীষ্মবর্ণন সমাপ্ত

* * *

The season that is fragrant with the trumpet flowers,
When lotus ponds entice and the melodious hours
Are sweet with one's beloved on a moonlit night –
May this, your summertime, be filled with all delight! (28)

Canto 2
The Rains

বর্ষা—ঋতুসংহার পৃ: ১৩

सशीकराम्भोधरमत्तकुञ्जरस्
तडित्पताकोऽशनिशब्दमर्दलः ।
समागतो राजवदुद्धतद्युतिर्
घनागमः कामिजनप्रियः प्रिये ॥ १॥

* * *

নিবিড় কান্তি ভরা সে প্রাবৃট
উদ্ধত রাজ, সমাগত হায় !
জল-কণা-বাহী বারিদ মত্ত-
মাতঙ্গ, তড়িৎ ধ্বজা-পট তায় ;
অশনি শব্দ মর্দল বাজে
রস-সিঞ্চিয়া জুড়ায় জীবন !
আসিলে নিকটে অবসান তাপ
হরণ করে গো প্রবাসীর মন ! ১

* * *

But now the air throbs as with a distant roar
    Of drums and lightning-banners stream above.
With storm-clouds for his elephants of war,
    Monsoon approaches like a king, my love! (1)

नितान्तनीलोत्पलपत्रकान्तिभिः
क्वचित्प्रभिन्नाञ्जनराशिसंनिभैः ।
क्वचित्सगर्भप्रमदास्तनप्रभैः
समाचितं व्योम घनैः समन्ततः ॥ २॥

* * *

নিতান্ত নীল কমল পত্র
গগনের শোভা ধরিয়াছে কভু;
কভু প্রভিন্ন অঞ্জনরাশি
প্রতিভার দ্যুতি ভরিয়াছে তবু,
এমনি বর্ণ খেলায় মাতিয়া
কত কি দেখায় দীপ্তিতে তারি,
সন্তানবতী পয়োধর ভার
প্রভারাজি হেন মেঘ বিস্তারি ! ২

* * *

Clouds dark as the blue lily which arrests
    With loveliness, or of a hue that vies
With nipples of a pregnant woman's breasts,
    Assemble now and occupy the skies. (2)

তৃষাকুলৈশ্চাতকপক্ষিণাং কুলৈঃ
প্রযাচিতাস্তোয়ভরাবলম্বিনঃ ।
প্রযান্তি মন্দং বহুধারবর্ষিণো
বলাহকাঃ শ্রোত্রমনোহরস্বনাঃ ॥ ৩ ॥

* * *

জল-ভারে হেরো প্রসারিত রহি
বহু ধারা তায় বর্ষণ দানি
শ্রুতি মনোহর স্বনিয়া তাহাতে
মন্দগতিতে যায় সে প্রয়াণি ;
চাতকের দল তৃষায় আকুল
যাচিছে তাহারা বারিরে তখন
হেরিয়া এ হেন বরষায় সখি,
কার বল এতে ভিজেনাগো মন ? ৩

* * *

Harmoniously they rumble through the air,
   Slow-moving, for with heavy loads they sink,
Showering their drops to grant the thirsty prayer
   Of *chatak* birds who have no other drink. (3)

बलाहकाश्वाशनिशब्दमर्दलाः
सुरेन्द्रचापं दधतस्तडिद्गुणम् ।
सुतीक्ष्णधारापतनोग्रसायकैस्
स्तुदन्ति चेतः प्रसभं प्रवासिनाम् ॥ ४॥

* * *

তড়িৎ-ইন্দ্র-ধনুর গুণেতে
প্রচণ্ড বাণ তীক্ষ্ণ ধারায়
বিঁধিছে বিরহী হৃদয়েতে লেগে
অশনি নিনাদ মাদল বাজায় ! ৪

* * *

Or marching off to battle to the beat
    Of thunder-drums, like warriors they dart
From rainbows strung with lightning a sharp sleet
    Of arrows at the traveller's lone heart. (4)

প্রভিন্নবৈদূর্যনিভৈস্তৃণাঙ্কুরৈः
    সমাচিতা প্রোথিতকন্দলীদলैः ।
বিভাতি শুক্লেতররত্নভূষিতা
    বরাঙ্গনেব ক্ষিতিরিন্দ্রগোপকैः ॥ ৫॥

* * *

বৈদূর্য্যের নীল মণি প্রভা
তৃণ-অঙ্কুরে ধরা বিদলিত ;
ইন্দ্রগোপ-কীট, কন্দলী
শ্যামল বরণ রতনে ভূষিত
বরাঙ্গনার রূপ ধরি রহে
মধুর ভঙ্গী মাধুর্য্য ভারে
তেমনি একালে দেখায় বিপুলা
বরণের শোভা বর্ষার ধারে ! ৫

* * *

Now, when the soil with emerald foliage teems
    And scarlet insects and with grasses blue
Like lapis lazuli, earth's body seems
    A lady's decked in gems of many a hue. (5)

सदा मनोज्ञं स्तनदुत्सवोत्सुकं
विकीर्णविस्तीर्णकलापशोभितम् ।
ससंभ्रमालिङ्गनचुम्बनाकुलं
प्रवृत्तनृत्यं कुलमद्य बर्हिणाम् ॥ ६॥

* * *

ময়ূর শোভিত কলাপের ভারে
বিসারী ত্রস্ত আলিঙ্গনেতে,
চুম্বনে ভরি মধুর নিনাদে
সুখ-বিমোহিত নৃত্যেতে মেতে ! ৬

* * *

Shrill heralds of the season of the rains,
    Shrieking with an exuberant display
And riot of their long, outspreading trains,
    The peacocks have begun their dance today. (6)

নিপাতয়ন্ত্যঃ পরিতস্তটদ্রুমান্
    প্রবৃদ্ধবেগৈঃ সলিলৈরনির্মলৈঃ ।
স্ত্রিয়ঃ সুদুষ্টা ইব জাতবিভ্রমাঃ
    প্রযান্তি নদ্যস্ত্বরিতং পয়োনিধিম্ ॥ ৭॥

* * *

প্রবৃদ্ধি বেগে কলুষিত নীরে
তটের বিটপী নিপতিত করে
দুষ্টা-রমণী-জাত-বিভ্রমে
ত্বরা গতি নদী ধাইছে সাগরে ! ৭

* * *

The turbid waters of the rivers race,
    Crumbling their banks with crash of toppling trees,
Like women gone astray who bring disgrace
    To all their kinsfolk, headlong to the seas. (7)

तृणोत्करैरुद्भतकोमलाङ्ग्रैश्
चितानि नीलैर्हरिणीमुखक्षतैः ।
वनानि वैन्ध्यानि हरन्ति मानसं
विभूषितान्युद्भतपल्लवैर्द्रुमैः ॥ ८॥

* * *

নব-কিশলয় ভূষিত তরুর
বিন্ধ্যা গিরির বনানীর তলে,
বিচিত্র নীল রঙের মায়ায়
হরিণেরা মুখে তৃণ ল'য়ে চলে ! ৮

* * *

Look, where the sprouting grass's tender blades
    Are nibbled by the deer and every hill
Bursts with new leaves! Now Vindhya's verdant glades
    And flowering forests make the senses thrill. (8)

विलोलनेत्रोत्पलशोभिताननै-
र्मृगैः समन्तादुपजातसाध्वसैः ।
समाचिता सैकतिनी वनस्थली
समुत्सुकत्वं प्रकरोति चेतसः ॥ ९ ॥

* * *

চঞ্চল আঁখি উৎপল-শোভা
ভয়াতুর মৃগ ধায় সঞ্চরি
বন-সৈকতে বেগে যেথা সেথা
দেখে মনে আনে ব্যাকুলতা তারি ! ৯

* * *

Startled, their large eyes trembling in alarm
    Like quivering lotus petals, graceful does,
Surprised in a sandy clearing, touch and charm
    The mind with memories of eyes like those. (9)

अभीक्ष्णमुच्चैर्ध्वनता पयोमुचा
  घनान्धकारीकृतशर्वरीष्वपि ।
तडित्प्रभादर्शितमार्गभूमयः
  प्रयान्ति रागादभिसारिकाः स्त्रियः ॥ १० ॥

* * *

পয়োদ যদিও ঘনান্ধকারী
শর্ব্বরী ভরে গরজন রবে
অনুরাগে নারী অভিসারে যায়
দামিনী-কিরণে পথ দেখি সাবে । ১০

* * *

Even though bellowing clouds engulf the night
  In inky blackness, yet a woman rash
With ardor hastens to the trysting site,
  Her road lit briefly by the lightning's flash. (10)

पयोधरैर्भीमगभीरनिस्वनैस्
    तडिद्भिरुद्वेजितचेतसो भृशम् ।
कृतापराधानपि योषितः प्रियान्
    परिष्वजन्ते शयने निरन्तरम् ॥ ११ ॥

* * *

ভীষণ গভীর নিনাদে জলদ
তড়িৎ হানিয়া উদ্বেগ আনে,
পর-বনিতায়ে হেরেছে যে পতি
আলিঙ্গনেতে জুড়ায় শয়ানে ! ১১

* * *

Her back turned to a husband who has erred,
    When suddenly the lightning bolt strikes fear
Into her heart and thunder's clap is heard,
    The wife forgives his faults and holds him near. (11)

विलोचनेन्दीवरवारिबिन्दभिर्
    निषिक्तबिम्बाधरचारुपल्लवाः ।
निरस्तमाल्याभरणानुलेपनाः
    स्थिता निराशाः प्रमदाः प्रवासिनाम् ॥ १२ ॥

* * *

বিরহিনী নারী মালা আভরণ
অনুলেপনেরে দেহে নাহি ধরে
লোচন-ইন্দীবর হ'তে বারি
চারু-কিশলয়-বিম্ব-অধরে
বিগলি সিক্ত করি ল'য়ে দুখে,
নিরাশা আকুল বিয়োগ বিধুর !
মনে ব্যাথা তার সদা ভরি রয়
এমনি প্রাবৃটে পতি রহি দূর ! ১২

* * *

Big drops appear in lotus eyes and spill
    On the soft lips of travellers' wives, who wear
No garlands now or jewelry, but still
    Watch for their husbands, staving off despair. (12)

বিপত্রপুষ্পাং নলিনীং সমুৎসুকা
বিহায় ভৃঙ্গাঃ শ্রুতিহারিনিস্বনাঃ ।
পতন্তি মূঢ়াঃ শিখিনাং প্রনৃত্যতাং
কলাপচক্রেষু নবোৎপলাশয়া ॥ ১৪ ॥

* * *

পাণ্ডু বরণ কীট, রজ, তৃণে
নব জলধারে ভূমিতলে তায়
সর্পের মত কুটিল গতিতে
প্রয়াণি নিম্নে বিসর্পি ধায় ;
মণ্ডূককুল অতি ভয়ে ভয়ে
দর্শন করি কম্পিত হিয়া
ভাবে কিয়ে মনে, বরষার দিনে
কাটিবে কি সুখে এমনি রহিয়া ?   ১৩

* * *

Grey with their loads of insects, dirt and weeds,
   Down the dry hillside new-born rivulets go,
Winding with a snakelike motion that misleads
   The frogs, who hop aside from their old foe. (13)

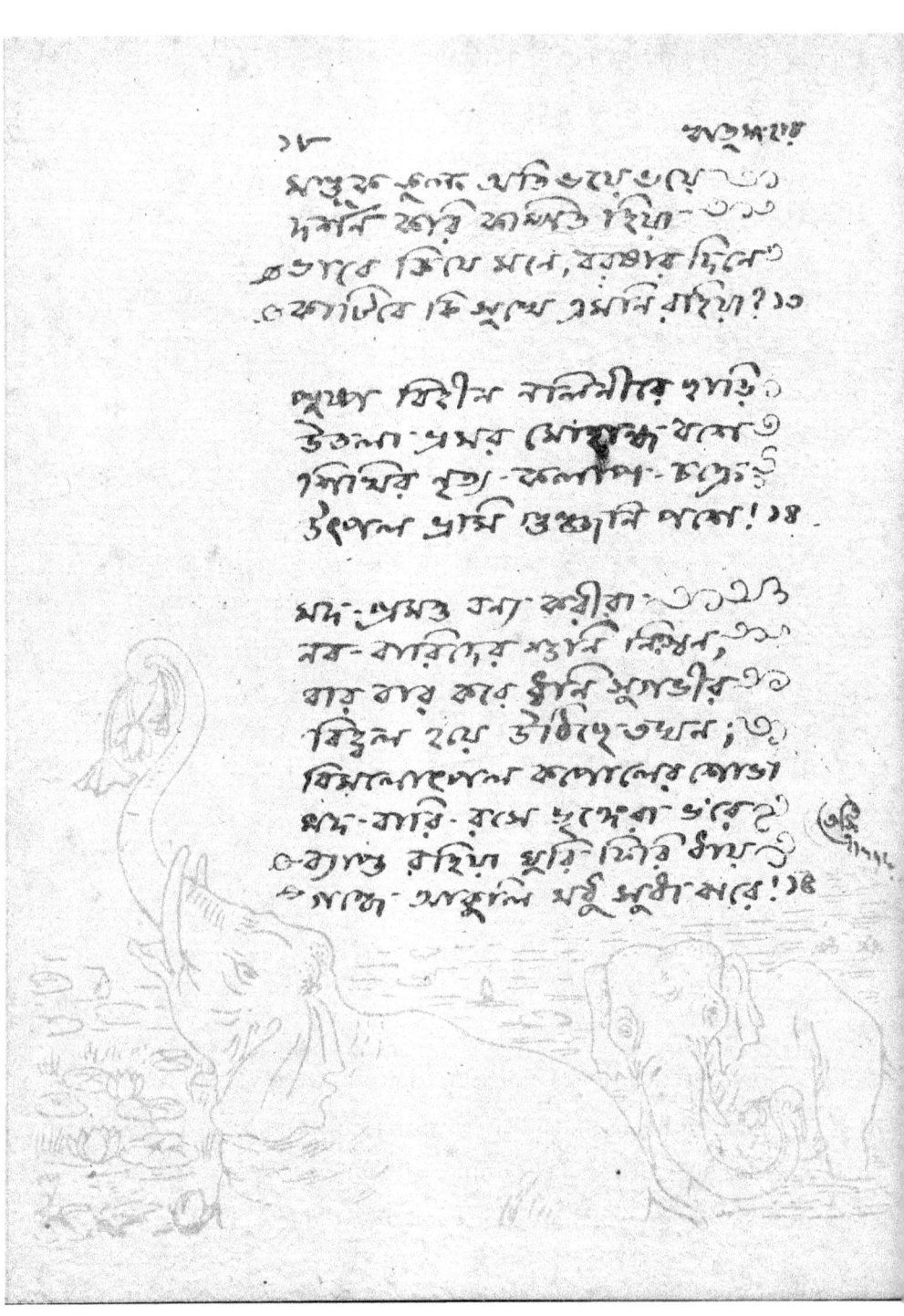

মধুকর তুলনা পতিভক্ষে যবে
দুর্শন সহি কামট হিয়া
তোমারে কিসে মনে, বরষব দিলে
কেমনে কি সুখে এমনি রহিয়া?১৩

সুখম বিহীন কমলিনীর হৃদে
উতলা ভ্রমর মোহন মেলি
পশিয়া পূন কমল-চরে
উড়িল তুমি তজ্ঞানি পরে!১৪

মদ-প্রমত্ত ঘন করীরা
নব-বারির শুনি কিশন,
বায় বয় কর ধ্বনি সুগভীর
বিছল হয়ে উঠিত তখন;
বিমলোৎপল কমলের তোড়া
মদ-বারি- রসে ধুইয়া ভরে
তুলিল রহিয়া ঘুরি নীরে ভাসি
লাজে অকুলি মধু সুধী সরে!১৫

विपत्रपुष्पां नलिनीं समुत्सुका
विहाय भृङ्गाः श्रुतिहारिनिस्वनाः ।
पतन्ति मूढाः शिखिनां प्रनृत्यतां
कलापचक्रेषु नवोत्पलाशया ॥ १४ ॥

* * *

পুষ্প বিহীন নলিনীরে ছাড়ি
উতলা ভ্রমর মহান্ধ বশে
শিখির নৃত্য কলাপ-চক্রে
উৎপল ভ্রমি গুঞ্জনি পশে ! ১৪

* * *

Murmuring past a lotus that has shed
    Its petals, eager swarms of bees assail,
Deluded by the vivid tints, instead
    The circles on a dancing peacock's tail. (14)

वनद्विपानां नववारिदस्वनैर्
    मदान्वितानां ध्वनतां मुहुर्मुहुः ।
कपोलदेशा विमलोत्पलप्रभाः
    सभृङ्गयूथैर्मदवारिभिध्रिताः ॥ १५॥

* * *

মদ-প্রমত্ত বন্য করীরা
নব-বারিদের শুনি নিঃস্বন,
বার বার করে ধ্বনি সুগভীর
বিহ্বল হ'য়ে উঠিছে তখন;
বিমলোৎপল কপোলের শোভা
মদ-বারি-রসে ভৃঙ্গেরা ভ'রে
ব্যাপ্ত রহিয়া ঘুরি ফিরি ধায়
গন্ধে আকুলি মধু সুধা ঝরে ! ১৫

* * *

Trumpeting in defiance at a cloud,
    Its thunderous rival, a wild elephant showers
Sweet streams of ichor, drawing bees to crowd
    Its temples dripping like blue lotus flowers. (15)

सितोत्पलाभाम्बुदचुम्बितोपलाः
    समाचिताः प्रस्रवणैः समन्ततः ।
प्रवृत्तनृत्यैः शिखिभिः समाकुलाः
    समुत्सुकत्वं जनयन्ति भूधराः ॥ १६ ॥

* * *

ঝরণা ধারায় ঘেরিয়া ভূধর
শিখীর নৃত্যে চল-চঞ্চল
উপলেরে চুমি দ্যুতি পায় যেন
গলদপটলে সিত-উৎপল ! ১৬

* * *

White, drifting clouds that kiss the rocky heights,
    The sparkle of the plunging waterfalls,
The pageant of the peacocks – these are sights
    One who has seen these mountains long recalls. (16)

कदम्बसर्जार्जुनकेतकीवनं
विकम्पयंस्तत्कुसुमाधिवासितः ।
सशीकराम्भोधरसङ्गशीतलः
समीरणः कं न करोति सोत्सुकम् ॥ १७ ॥

* * *

জল-শীকরেতে সিক্ত মেঘের
সঙ্গ শীতল সমীরণ সাথে
শাল, অর্জুন, কেতকী, কদম
গন্ধ কাঁপনে কেই বা না মাতে ? ১৭

* * *

Now, when the scents of many flowering trees
   Are wafted through the land and rains impart
Exhilarating freshness to the breeze,
   Who can remain the master of his heart? (17)

শিরোরুহৈঃ শ্রোণিতটাবলম্বিভিঃ
    কৃতাবতংসৈঃ কুসমৈঃ সুগন্ধিভিঃ ।
স্তনৈঃ সহারৈর্বদনৈঃ সসীধুভিঃ
    স্ত্রিয়ো রতিং সংজনয়ন্তি কামিনাম্ ॥ ১৮ ॥

* * *

শ্রোণিতট লটি অলক সুঠাম,
সুগন্ধি ফুল, কানের ভূষণ
স্রক্-চন্দন বক্ষ ভারেতে
শীধু-মধু ভরা চন্দ্র বদন !
বর্ষার দিনে রমণীয় ধরে
রমণীর রূপ, জীবন জুড়ায় !
শোভায় তাহার নেহারি পুলকে
প্রিয়জন-মন খুসি করে তায় ! ১৮

* * *

Long hair cascading on their sloping hips,
    Flowers worn as fragrant earrings, lustrous pearls
Upon the bosom and wine-moistened lips
    Enhance the witchery of lovely girls. (18)

तडिल्लताशक्रधनुर्विभूषिताः
पयोधरास्तोयभरावलम्बिनः ।
स्त्रियश्च काञ्चीमणिकुण्डलोज्ज्वला
हरन्ति चेतो युगपत्प्रवासिनाम् ॥ १९ ॥

* * *

তড়িৎলতায় রামধনু রঙে
রাঙাইয়া মেঘ জলভারে নত,
কাঞ্চী, মণির কুণ্ডলোজ্জ্বল
রমণীরা মন হরিছে গো কত ! ১৯

* * *

But when the traveller sees the lightning-streak
    In heaven and the rainbow's rich array,
Reminded of his love, his limbs grow weak –
    Her girdle's flash and jewelled earrings' play. (19)

मालाः कदम्बनवकेसरकेतकीभिर्
   आयोजिताः शिरसि बिभ्रति योषितोऽद्य ।
कर्णान्तरेषु ककुभद्रुममञ्जरीभिर्
   इच्छानुकूलरचितानवतंसकाश्च ॥ २० ॥

* * *

যুবতীরা শিরে শোভিছে কদম
কেতকী বকুলে নিজমনে গড়ি
গাঁথি মালা হার, কুকুভ তরুর
সঞ্চারী কানে ভূষণেরে পরি ! ২০

* * *

The many-colored blossoms of the hour
   In garlands gracing women's heads appear,
Except the clusters of the *kakubh* flower,
   Reserved as dainty pendants for the ear. (20)

কালাগুরুপ্রচুরচন্দনচর্চিতাঙ্গ্যঃ
পুষ্পাবতংসসুরভীকৃতকেশপাশাঃ ।
শ্রুত্বা ধ্বনিং জলমুচাং ত্বরিতং প্রদোষে
শয্যাগৃহং গুরুগৃহাত্প্রবিশন্তি নার্যঃ ॥ ২১ ॥

* * *

প্রচুর অগুরু চন্দন শোভা
পয়োদ ধ্বনিরে শুনিয়া সে নারী
গুরুজন ঘর হইতে শয়নে
প্রদোষে ত্বরায় যাইলে তাহারি
ফুলে পড়া হার, কর্ণ ভূষণে
গন্ধ আমোদে কেশপাশ মাতে
সুখের নিদান কি আছেগো আর
বরষার গুণ প্রকাশিছে তাতে । ২১

* * *

Her body redolent of sandal paste,
    Hair decked with flowers that shed a sweet perfume,
When evening thunder moans, the wife in haste
    Slips from her elders to her husband's room. (21)

कुवलयदलनीलैरुन्नतैस्तोयनम्रैर्
मृदुपवनविधूतैर्मन्दमन्दं चलद्भिः ।
अपहृतमिव चेतस्तोयदैः सेन्द्रचापैः
पथिकजनवधूनां तद्वियोगाकुलानाम् ॥ २२ ॥

* * *

নীল কুবলয় দলের মতন
জল ভারে নত লভি মৃদুগতি,
উন্নত রহি জলধর তবে
পবন কাঁপায়ে সুমন্দ অতি
বিয়োগ বিধুর বিরহিনী বধূ
ইন্দ্রধনুতে সজ্জিত মেঘে
নেহারিয়া মন করিছে হরণ
বাদলেতে আরি ছবি রয় জেগে ! ২২॥

* * *

Huge shapes of dusky blue above the rainbow's arch,
High water-burdened clouds in their slow, stately march
Are followed by the tearful gaze of wives who yearn
Toward lands from which their loved ones still do not return.

(22)

मुदित इव कदम्बैर्जातपुष्पैः समन्तात्
    पवनचलितशाखैः शाखिभिर्नृत्यतीव ।
हसितमिव विधत्ते सूचिभिः केतकीनां
    नवसलिलनिषेकच्छिन्नतापो वनान्तः ॥ २३॥

* * *

নব-বারিধারা সেচনেতে তাপ
বন বনান্তে লইতেছে হরি
বিকসিয়া নব কদম কুসুমে
পুলক উদয়ে রোমাঞ্চ ধরি
বায়ু ভরে তরু শাখারে দোলায়ে
নৃত্যের ভাব আনে দেখি মনে
কেতকীর ফুলে কাটার বিকাশে ;
হাসিটি দেখায় অধরের কোণে ! ২৩

* * *

Bristling as if for joy with blossoms everywhere,
Waving as in a dance their branches in the air,
Laughing with the white buds the screwpine groves display,
The forests hail the quenching of the heat today. (23)

शिरसि बकुलमालां मालतीभिः समेतां
विकसितनवपुष्पैर्यूथिकाकुड्मलैश्च ।
विकचनवकदम्बैः कर्णपूरं वधूनां
रचयति जलदौघः कान्तवत्काल एषः ॥ २४ ॥

* * *

জলধর তায় বল্লভ প্রায়
মালতীর সাথে গাঁথি বকুলেতে
কামিনী কবরী শোভিয়া ভূষণে
বিকট-নবীন-কদম কানেতে
যূথিকা পুষ্প মুকুলেতে নব
রচনা করিয়া সাজাইয়া তুলি
ভরে সুখে সদা প্রেমের পরশে
হরষে হৃদয় উঠিতেছে দুলি ! ২৪

* * *

The season of the rainclouds with a lover's zest
Weaves garlands for the heads of maidens flowing-tressed
With *bakul* blooms and buds of jasmine intermixed,
While on the ear the fresh *kadamba* flower is fixed. (24)

দধতি বরকুচাগ্রৈরুন্নতৈর্হারযষ্টিং
প্রতনুসিতদুকূলান্যায়তৈঃ শ্রোণিবিম্বৈঃ ।
নবজলকণসেকাদুদ্গতাং রোমরাজিং
ললিতবলিবিভঙ্গৈর্মধ্যদেশৈশ্চ নার্যঃ ॥ ২৫॥

* * *

গুরু-নিতম্ব শোভিত রয়েছে
চিকন ধবল ঢাকি বসনেতে
পীন বর্তুল বক্ষেতে হার
ললিত কটির বলি বিভাগেতে
মুকুতার মত শত রাশি রাশি
নব-জল-কণা প্রবেশিয়া ফুটি
মোহিনীর রূপ ধারণ করিছে
তাহাতে তখন রোমাঞ্চি উঠি ! ২৫

* * *

Pearls nestle on their breasts and dangle from the tips;
Thin robes reveal the rounded outlines of their hips;
While just below the navel, wispy lines of hair
Rise thrilling at the touch of coolness in the air. (25)

নবজলকণসঙ্গাচ্ছীততামাদধানঃ
কুসুমভরনতানাং লাসকঃ পাদপানাম্ ।
জনিতরুচিরগন্ধঃ কেতকীনাং রজোভিঃ
পরিহরতি নভস্বান্প্রোষিতানাং মনাংসি ॥ ২৬॥

* * *

কুসুমের ভারে অবনত তরু
নব-জল-কণা সঙ্গ লভিয়া
সুশীতল করি কেতকী কুসুমে
যায় সেথা হিম সমীর বহিয়া ;
পরাগ রেণুর রুচির গন্ধে
মাতিয়া তুলিছে কুঞ্জ কানন !
এহেন বরষা প্রিয়া কাছে নাই
উদাস করিছে প্রবাসীর মন ! ২৬

* * *

Partaking of the freshness of the fleeting showers,
Frolicking in the boughs which overflow with flowers
And laden with the screwpine's pungency, the breeze
Torments the hearts of parted lovers with unease. (26)

जलभरनमितानामाश्रयोऽस्माकमुच्चैर्
अयमिति जलसेकैस्तोयदास्तोयनम्राः ।
अतिशयपरुषाभिर्ग्रीष्मवह्नेः शिखाभिः
समुपजनिततापं ह्लादयन्तीव विन्ध्यम् ॥ २७ ॥

* * *

গ্রীষ্ম-বহ্নি-পরুষ শিখায়
তাপ উপজিয়া বিন্ধ্য গিরিরে
হেরিয়া জলদ জলভারে নত
সিক্ত নম্র করিয়া সুধীরে
আশ্রম তারি ভরিয়া আপন
বারিধারা ঢালি প্রীতিভরি তায়
প্রাবৃট কালেতে এমনি সে রীতি
সুখেতে বিহারী মাদল বাজায় ! ২৭

* * *

Today at last this lofty Vindhya, vexed so much
By cruel fires which held his forests in their clutch,
He on whose heights the rainclouds rest and are renewed,
Is recompensed by them with showers of gratitude. (27)

बहुगुणरमणीयः कामिनीचित्तहारी
    तरुविटपलतानां बान्धवो निर्विकारः ।
जलदसमय एष प्राणिनां प्राणभूतो
    दिशतु तव हितानि प्रायशो वाञ्छितानि ॥ २८ ॥

इति प्रावृड्वर्णनं नाम द्वितीयः सर्गः ॥

* * *

হে শখা, দেখ গো, প্রাবৃট একাল
রমণীয় বহু গুণে গুণময়
তরুলতা তারে বান্ধব করে
কামিনী জনার মন হরি লয় !
প্রাণীর সে প্রাণ জলের ধারায়
বিকার বিহীন তাহাতে প্রকাশি
করুক সফল জীবন তোমার
বহু বাঞ্ছিত হিত ল'য়ে আসি ! ২৮

বর্ষাবর্ণন সমাপ্ত

* * *

Season of many charms when women lose their hearts,
When woodlands sway and blossom and the heat departs,
The gladdener of creatures – may this time of rain
Satisfy all desires your mind may entertain! (28)

Canto 3
Autumn

শরৎ—ঋতুসংহার পৃঃ ২৫

কাশাংশুকা বিকচপদ্মমনোজ্ঞবক্ত্রা
সোন্মাদহংসরবনূপুরনাদরম্যা ।
আপক্কশালিরুচিরানতগাত্রযষ্টিঃ
প্রাপ্তা শরন্নববধূরিব রূপরম্যা ॥ ১ ॥

* * *

শরতের রূপ রমণীয় অতি
নববধূ বেশে সমাগত সুখে
কাশ-অংশুক ধারণ করিয়া
বিরচ-কমল মনোজ্ঞ মুখে
পক্ক-ধান্য চারু-তনু-রুচি
মত্ত-হংস নিনাদ নূপুর
কমনীয় সাজে সেজেছে ধরণী
পেলব কোমল দুখ হয় দূর ! ১

* * *

Wearing as her white gown the grasses' wind-blown fleece,
Her anklet bells resounding in the call of geese,
Her slender form in stalks of ripening grain descried,
Autumn has come in all her splendor like a bride! (1)

তৃতীয় সর্গ

শরৎবর্ণন

শরতের রূপ রমণীয় অতি
নবরূপী বেশে সমাগত সুখে
বরষা-অশুভক বীরণ কাশীর -
বিকশিত-কমল শালোক মুখে
শঙ্খ-ধ্বনি চক্র তনু কটি
মত-২য় স নিনাদি নূপুর
রমনীয় সাজে সেজেছে ধরনী-
পেঁজা তুলার ছেঁড়া মেঘ দূরে !

ধরনী কাননে তরু মাঝিয়া -
যজ্ঞী চন্দ্র-কিরন-শীকরে
নদী জলে হংস, সরসী কুমুদ,
সপ্তপর্ণী-অরণ্য ঘিরে

काशैर्मही शिशिरदीधितिना रजन्यो
    हंसैर्जलानि सरितां कुमुदैः सरांसि ।
सप्तच्छदैः कुसुमभारनतैर्वनान्ताः
    शुक्लीकृतान्युपवनानि च मालतीभिः ॥ २॥

* * *

ধরণী কাশের গুচ্ছে সাজিয়া
রজনী চন্দ্র কিরণ শীকরে
নদী জলে হাঁস, সরসী কুমুদে,
সপ্তপর্ণী অরণ্যে ধরে
কুসুমের ভারে অবনত রহি ;
উপবনতল শ্বেত মালতীতে
শুক্ল আভাসে দশ দিশি ভাসে
সবাকার মন হরণ করিতে ! ২

* * *

The moon pours down at night a luster white and cool;
Now swans and waterlilies brighten every pool;
The woods grow white with throngs of *saptaparna* flowers,
And gleaming white with jasmine are the pleasure bowers. (2)

চञ्चन्मनोज्ञशफरीरसनाकलापाः
पर्यन्तसंस्थितसिताण्डजपङ्क्तिहाराः ।
नद्यो विशालपुलिनान्तनितम्बबिम्बा
मन्दं प्रयान्ति समदाः प्रमदा इवाद्य ॥ ३॥

* * *

যৌবন-মদ-গরবী প্রমদা
মন্দ মন্দ গতি হেন নদী
মধুর চপল শফরী রসনা
বহি চলে ধীরে সদা নিরবধি !
প্রান্তেতে তার ধবল মরাল
বিহঙ্গকুল হারের আভায়
বিশাল বিপুল তট-নিতম্ব
ধরিছে জগৎ শরৎ-শোভায় ! ৩

* * *

Swinging her sparkling girdle in the minnows' splash,
Banks lined with birds whose whiteness is her necklace' flash,
The river with her spreading hips of golden sand
Glides dreaming like a lovesick maiden through the land. (3)

व्योम क्वचिद्रजतशङ्खमृणालगौरस्
 त्यक्ताम्बुभिर्लघुतया शतशः प्रयातैः ।
संलक्ष्यते पवनवेगचलैः पयोदै
 राजेव चामरशतैरुपवीज्यमानः ॥ ४ ॥

* * *

রজত-শঙ্খ মৃণাল ধবল
বারিহীন মেঘ ধরে লঘু ভার,
প্রয়াণি পবন শত দিকে ধায়
চামরে ব্যজিত রাজার বাহার
গগনের ভাতি, দেখে মনে হয়
বিভাবটি ল'য়ে বিপুল সে তার
এমনি শরতে ধরণী ধরেছে
প্রেমিক-মোহন চিত্ত উদার ! ৪

* * *

As breezes stir a myriad cloud-puffs rendered light
By dropping of their waters, fine and silver-white,
The sky looks like a pompous king whose royal flesh
Attendants with a hundred yak-tail fans refresh. (4)

भिन्नाञ्जनप्रचयकान्ति नभो मनोज्ञं
बन्धूकपुष्परजसाऽरुणिता च भूमिः ।
वप्राश्च पक्वकलमावृतभूमिभागाः
प्रोत्कण्ठयन्ति न मनो भुवि कस्य यूनः ॥ ५॥

* * *

দলিত অঁজন চিকন শোভন
মধুর সে রূপ-কান্তিতে নভে
বন্ধুক ফুলে রচিত অরুণ
পক্বধান্যে ভরা ক্ষেত যবে
প্রকৃতির শোভা হেরে কোন্ যুবা-
হৃদয়ে না ভ'রে ব্যথা নিদারুণ
এহেন কালের অনুভূতি ভরি
জেগে রয় ল'য়ে ভাব সকরুণ ! ৫

* * *

When heaven's azure deepens to the hue of ground
Collyrium, when red pollen scatters all around,
Blown from *bandhuka* flowers, and fields are emerald green,
What youthful heart brims not with longing at the scene? (5)

মন্দানিলাকুলিতচারুতরাগ্রশাখঃ
পুষ্পোদ্গমপ্রচয়কোমলপল্লবাগ্রঃ ।
মত্তদ্বিরেফপরিপীতমধুপ্রসেকশ্
চিত্তং বিদারয়তি কস্য ন কোবিদারঃ ॥ ৬॥

* * *

শাখাগ্রে চারু-সুধীর সমীরে
আকুলিত রহে পাদপ সেথায় ;
পল্লব চূড়া পুষ্প উদয়ে
অতীব পেলব রূপের বিভায়,
মত্ত ভ্রমর মকরন্দের
রস করিপান তখন যাহার
কাঞ্চন তরু কাহার না আনে
এহেন কালেতে হৃদয় বিকার ! ৬

* * *

Its branches troubled gently by the wind's caress,
Luring intoxicated swarms of bees to press
Among the nectar-trickling blossoms that unfold,
The *kovidara* tree is something to behold. (6)

तारागणप्रवरभूषणमुद्वहन्ती
मेघावरोधपरिमुक्तशशाङ्कवक्त्रा ।
ज्योत्स्नादुकूलममलं रजनी दधाना
वृद्धिं प्रयात्यनुदिनं प्रमदेव बाला ॥ ७ ॥

* * *

রজনী আরকা ভূষণে সাজিয়া
বিমল-চাঁদিনী-কোমল বসনে
তরুণ প্রমদা অনুদিন বাড়ে
সরাইয়া মেঘ ইন্দু বদনে ! ৭

* * *

Resplendent with her starry ornaments, the night,
Whose shining face, the moon, no clouds withhold from sight,
Robed in pure moonlight, grows in loveliness each day,
Like a young girl whose charms increase in every way. (7)

कारण्डवाननविघट्टितवीचिमालाः
कादम्बसारसकुलाकुलतीरदेशाः ।
कुर्वन्ति हंसविरुतैः परितो जनस्य
प्रीतिं सरोरुहरजोरुणितास्तटिन्यः ॥ ८ ॥

* * *

পদ্মপরাগে তটিনী আকুল
হংস-নিনাদ সুধা রসে ভুলি
প্রীতির উদয় করি সবাকার
চঞ্চু আঘাতে তরঙ্গ তুলি
বালিহাঁস আর সরস মিথুনে
তীরদেশ ভরি রাখিয়াছে সেথা
শোভা যা ধরিছে শুভ্র বিমল
শরতের রূপ বর্ণিবে কে তা ? ৮

* * *

Wild ducks that dive their heads beneath the ripples, pink
Flamingoes and white cranes that crowd the water's brink,
The music of the swans – what words are there to praise
The beauty of the rivers in these autumn days? (8)

नेत्रोत्सवो हृदयहारिमरीचिमालः
प्रह्लादकः शिशिरशीकरवारिवर्षी ।
पत्युर्वियोगविषदिग्धशरक्षतानां
चन्द्रो दहत्यतितरां तनुमङ्गनानाम् ॥ ९॥

* * *

আঁখি-উৎসব চিত্তহরণ
মরীচি মালায় সুশোভার ভারে
খুসি ভরা চাঁদ, শীতল কিরণে
বর্ষণ করি সুমধুর ধারে,
পতি-বিরহের বিষজ্বালা শর-
ক্ষত দেহটিরে জ্বালি করে ক্ষয় !
এহেন দিনেতে যদি চিরতরে
পতি সাথে ভাবে মিলন না হয় ? ৯॥

* * *

When the moon floats through heaven garlanded with beams
And gladdens every eye, that shower of coolness seems
To separated lovers like a fiery rain
Of poisoned darts that only aggravates their pain. (9)

आकम्पयन्फलभरानतशालिजाला-
न्यानर्तयंस्तरुवरान्कुसुमावनम्रान् ।
उत्फुल्लपङ्कजवनां नलिनीं विधुन्वन्
यूनां मनश्चलयति प्रसभं नभस्वान् ॥ १० ॥

* * *

ফসলে আনত ধান্যের ক্ষেতে
সমীরণ বহি হিল্লোলি ধায়,
কুসুমের ভারে অবনত তরু
বিকশিত করি অরণ্যে তায়,
ফুল্ল কমল সরসীর বুকে
চল-চঞ্চলি দেয় তারি নীর !
এমনি একালে সকলি শোভন
যুবকের মন করিছে অধীর ! ১০

* * *

Ripe, burdened stalks are dancing in the paddy field
While, wrestling with the wind, the tree-tops toss and yield;
A vivid wave of petals is the lotus pond –
When Nature is astir, what heart will not respond? (10)

সোন্মাদহংসমিথুনৈরুপশোভিতানি
	স্বচ্ছপ্রফুল্লকমলোৎপলভূষিতানি ।
মন্দপ্রভাতপবনোদ্ধৃতবীচিমালা-
	ন্যুৎকণ্ঠয়ন্তি সহসা হৃদয়ং সরাংসি ॥ ১১ ॥

* * *

প্রমত্ত-কল-হংস মিথুন
স্বস্থ-ফুল্ল কমলোৎপলে
ভূষিত মন্দ প্রভাত পবনে
তরঙ্গমালা সরোবর জলে
ভ্রমিতে হেরিলে মনেতে সবার
যেন কিযে এক ব্যথা ভরিআনে
পথিক জনার বিরহ দিবসে
বিচ্ছেদ দুখ ঢালি দেয় প্রাণে ! ১১

* * *

Graceful with gliding couples of enamored swans,
Mirroring brilliant flowers and shimmering in the dawns
When ruffled by a breath of air – the senses ache
With longing near the stillness of an autumn lake. (11)

नष्टं धनुर्बलभिदो जलदोदरेषु
    सौदामिनी स्फुरति नाद्य वियत्पताका ।
धुन्वन्ति पक्षपवनैर्न नभो बलाकाः
    पश्यन्ति नोन्नतमुखा गगनं मयूराः ॥ १२ ॥

* * *

ইন্দ্রধনুটি জলদ উদরে
চমকেনা আর বিজলী পতাকা
শিখী উচা মুখে হেরেনা শূন্যে
কাঁপেনা আকাশ পক্ষে বলাকা ! ১২

* * *

Now one forgets the rainbow's hues, the thunder's crash
And lightning-banners streaming in the storm-winds' clash;
Nor do migrating cranes flap now their wings above,
Or peacocks lift their heads to greet the clouds they love. (12)

नृत्यप्रयोगरहितांस्त्रिखिनो विहाय
हंसानुपैति मदनो मधुरप्रगीतान् ।
मुक्त्वा कदम्बकुटजार्जुनसर्जनीपान्
सप्तच्छदानुपगता कुसुमोद्रमश्रीः ॥ १३ ॥

* * *

মদন নৃত্য-রহিত ময়ূরে
ত্যজিয়া হংসসুমধুর গীতি
শ্রবণ করিতে রত হন তবে
বাড়ায়ে তাদের হৃদয়ের প্রীতি !
কুসুম ফোটার শোভাটি এখন
অর্জুন, শাল, কুটজেরে ছাড়ি
করিছে গ্রহণ সপ্তপর্ণী
প্রকাশিয়া আভা সান্দ্র তারি ! ১৩

* * *

The rapture that inspired the peacock's dance has gone
Today into the dulcet singing of the swan.
The *kakubh* and *kadamba* trees no longer house
The Blossom Queen, who seeks the *saptaparna* boughs. (13)

शेफालिकाकुसुमगन्धमनोहराणि
स्वस्थस्थिताण्डजकुलप्रतिनादितानि ।
पर्यन्तसंस्थितमृगीनयनोत्पलानि
प्रोत्कण्ठयन्त्युपवनानि मनांसि पुंसाम् ॥ १४ ॥

* * *

শেফালি কুসুম গন্ধ মোহন
বিহঙ্গ স্থির রহি দলে দলে,
কলগীতি ভরি প্রতিধ্বনিতে,
প্রান্ত মৃগের নয়নোৎপলে,
মঞ্জুল উপবনেরে নেহারি
উৎকণ্ঠায় বাড়ায় বিকার ;
ভাবিয়া হৃদয়ে সুখ বেদনাতে
এমন দিনেতে শরতে সবার ! ১৪

* * *

Starlike, the exquisite *shephalika* flowers scent
Delightful parks resounding with the merriment
Of birds of many voices, where one may surprise
Does browsing tranquilly with large and timid eyes. (14)

कह्लारपद्मकुमुदानि मुहुर्विधुन्वंस्
तत्सङ्गमादधिकशीतलतामुपेतः ।
उत्कण्ठयत्यतितरां पवनः प्रभाते
पत्रान्तलग्नतुहिनाम्बुविधूयमानः ॥ १५॥

* * *

সমীর কুমুদ পদ্ম শালুকে
বার বার ভরি হিল্লোলি ধীরে
সঙ্গ তাদের লভিয়া শীতল
পত্র অন্তে তুহিনের নীরে
লগন যা' ছিল, ধৌত করিয়া
বহি যায় এই শরত প্রভাতে
বেদনাটি তায় সহজে বাড়ায়
হিম বায়ু দিয়া শীত আনি তাতে ! ১৫

* * *

At sunrise, a delicious breeze which stirs a pool
Of lotuses unfolding to the sunbeams, cool
And fragrant, animates the dewdrops with a slight
Caress that sets them trembling in the early light. (15)

সংপন্নশালিনিচয়াবৃতভূতলানি
স্বস্থস্থিতপ্রচুরগোকুলশোভিতানি ।
হংসৈঃ সসারসকুলৈঃ প্রতিনাদিতানি
সীমান্তরাণি জনয়ন্তি নৃণাং প্রমোদম্ ॥ ১৬ ॥

* * *

পাকা শালি ধানে বিছানো ধরণী
প্রচুর ধেনুর পালে ভরা থাকি
হংস সারস প্রতিধ্বনিতে
এমনি আকুলি চরাচর রাখি
সীমান্ত জনে প্রমোদে জাগায়
শরৎ আসিলে হরষেতে মাতি
সকলি সেথায় রুচি অনুপম
ধরিয়া রয়েছে সদা দিবারাতি ! ১৬

* * *

Fields dense with the luxuriance of the ripening grains,
Lakes that reverberate with calling geese and cranes,
Pastures where placid cows absorb the temperate sun
Make the autumnal landscape an entrancing one. (16)

हंसैर्जिता सुललिता गतिरङ्गनानाम्
    अम्भोरुहैर्विकसितैर्मुखचन्द्रकान्तिः ।
नीलोत्पलैर्मदकलानि विलोचनानि
    भ्रूविभ्रमाश्च रुचिरास्तनुभिस्तरङ्गैः ॥ १७॥

* * *

হংস করিছে অঙ্গনা জয়
অনুকারী তার সুললিত গতি
মুখ-চন্দ্রিমা বিকচ কমল
কল-তরঙ্গ সুন্দর অতি
এবিলাস-ভাষ দেয় তারি নীরে
নীল-উৎপল চাহনি সুনীল
বিকাশি ধরেছে নারী আঁখিটিরে
ভরিছে তাহারি শোভায় নিখিল ! ১৭

* * *

The swan's slow gait is like a woman's in its grace;
The lotuses are rivals of her perfect face;
Blue wind-tossed lilies vie with her alluring glance,
And her brows' supple play reflects the ripples' dance. (17)

শ্যামা লতাঃ কুসুমভারনতপ্রবালাঃ
স্ত্রীণাং হরন্তি ধৃতভূষণবাহুকান্তিম্ ।
দন্তাবভাসবিশদস্মিতচন্দ্রকান্তিং
কঙ্কেলিপুষ্পরুচিরা নবমালতী চ ॥ ১৮ ॥

* * *

কুসুমেতে নত পল্লবে ভরি
শ্যাম লতা তার বাহুর ভূষণ
ললনা শোভিছে কঙ্কেলি ফুলে
নব-মালতীরে করিয়া গ্রহণ
দন্তের প্রভা, লভি নির্মল
স্মিত-চন্দ্রের রূপ দ্যুতি ভায়
হরণ করিছে মনেরে শরত
অমল কান্তি সুবিমলতায় ! ১৮

* * *

Their twigs bent low with blossoms, creepers call to mind
Slim arms arrayed in jewelled bracelets, while entwined
White jasmine and the red *ashoka* flower eclipse
The sweetness of a smile that gleams from ruby lips. (18)

केशान्तिरान्तघननीलविकुञ्चिताग्रान्
आपूरयन्ति वनिता नवमालतीभिः ।
कर्णेषु च प्रवरकाञ्चनकुण्डलेषु
नीलोत्पलानि विविधानि निवेशयन्ति ॥ १९ ॥

* * *

বনিতারা ঘন নীল কুঞ্চিত
সুচারু অলকে মালতী মালায়
সোনার কর্ণ আভরণ পরি
বিবিধ নীলোৎপলে শোভে তায় ! ১৯

* * *

Girls lavish now, diffusing fragrance through the air,
Fresh jasmine on the flowing blackness of their hair
And, to accentuate their golden earrings, choose
To wear beside them lilies of the darkest hues. (19)

हारैः सचन्दनरसैः स्तनमण्डलानि
श्रोणीतटं सुविपुलं रसनाकलापैः ।
पादाम्बुजानि कलनूपुरशेखरैश्च
नार्यः प्रहृष्टमनसोऽद्य विभूषयन्ति ॥ २० ॥

* * *

রমণীরা আজি হরষে অধীর
স্রক্‌চন্দন ভরি লয়ে বুকে
কটি-মেখলায় গুরু নিতম্বে
কলপ্‌পুরেতে সাজিতেছে সুখে ! ২০

* * *

Necklaces draped on breasts enhanced with sandal paste,
Girdles whose bands are stretched below the slender waist,
The melody of anklet bells on dainty feet
Make the enchanting season's ornaments complete. (20)

স্ফুটকুমুদচিতানাং রাজহংসাশ্রিতানাং
মরকতমণিভাসা বারিণা ভূষিতানাম্ ।
শ্রিয়মতিশয়রূপাং ব্যোম তোয়াশয়ানাং
বহতি বিগতমেঘং চন্দ্রতারাবিকীর্ণম্ ॥ ২১ ॥

* * *

গগনে তরিছে চন্দ্র তারকা
মেঘহীন রহি কুসুমে বিকাশি ;
রাজহাঁসগুলি মরকত মণি
কান্তিতে ভরি রয়েছে প্রকাশি
বাপী নীরে ধরে নির্ম্মল ভাতি
আজি এই মধু শরতের দিনে
এহেন কালের রসভাবগুলি
লইবে রসিকা নাগরীরা চিনে ! ২১

* * *

The drifting moon and hosts of flickering stars that crowd
The loveliness of evening skies without a cloud
Are matched by day in lakes where flocking geese alight
And white blooms dot the water's emerald delight. (21)

শরদি কুমুদসঙ্গাহ্লাদ্যবো বান্তি শীতা
বিগতজলদবৃন্দা দিগ্বিভাগা মনোজ্ঞাঃ ।
বিগতকলুষমম্ভঃ শ্যানপঙ্কা ধরিত্রী
বিমলকিরণচন্দ্রং ব্যোম তারাবিচিত্রম্ ॥ ২২॥

* * *

কুসুমের ছোঁয়া লাগিয়া শীতল
বায়ু বহে আজি শরতের কালে
জলদের জালবৃন্দ বিগত
নির্ম্মল শোভা দশদিক ভালে
সুবিমল নীর শুষ্ক পঙ্ক
অমল ধবল কিরণের ধারা
ইন্দু সঙ্গ লভিয়া ধরেছে
বিচিত্র রূপ গগনের তারা ! ২২

* * *

Pleasurable is the breeze in autumn, fresh and cool
And scented with the flowers that smile in every pool;
The waters now are limpid and the land is dry,
The moon and stars majestic in a cloudless sky. (22)

दिवसकरमयूखैर्बोध्यमानं प्रभाते
वरयुवितमुखाभं पङ्कजं जृम्भतेऽद्य ।
कुमुदमपि गतेऽस्तं लीयते चन्द्रबिम्बे
हसितमिव वधूनां प्रोषितेषु प्रियेषु ॥ २३॥

* * *

দিন-কর করে বিমলপরভাতে
উল্লাসী দুলি বিকশি কমল
বর-যুবতীর বদন আভাতে
এমনি প্রকাশি ধরিয়াছে ছল !
শশির কিরণ গত যবে সেথা
কুমুদ, পথিক বধূ হেন তায়
বিরহ বিধুর রহি সেইক্ষণে
মলিন হাসিটি হাসিয়া পালায় ! ২৩

* * *

Touched by the sun's first rays, the lotus now expands
Like a sweet face awakened by a lover's hands;
But the night-lily's laughter ends in tears of dew
When, summoned by the dawn, her moon recedes from view. (23)

असितनयनलक्ष्मीं लक्षयित्वोत्पलेषु
    क्वणितकनककाञ्चीं मत्तहंसस्वनेषु ।
अधररुचिरशोभां बन्धुजीवे प्रियाणां
    पथिकजन इदानीं रोदिति भ्रान्तचित्तः ॥ २४॥

***

পথিকেরা হেরে উৎপল 'পরে
প্রিয়ার অসিত-লোচনের শোভা
হংএর কল-নিঃস্বনে শোনে
কনক-মেখলা ধ্বনি মনোলোভা !
কন্দুক ফুলে ওষ্ঠ রাঙানো
হেরিছে রমণী রহিয়াছে সাজি
ভাবিয়া তাহারা ভ্রান্ত মনেতে
করিছে রোদন শরতেতে আজি ! ২৪

***

The magic of an eye's dark curve looks from a lake
Of lilies at the traveller, or his ears mistake
A clamor of wild geese for bells on swaying hips,
Or crimson petals haunt his gaze like yearning lips. (24)

स्त्रीणां विहाय वदनेषु शशाङ्कलक्ष्मीं
काम्यं च हंसवचनं मणिनूपुरेषु ।
बन्धूककान्तिमधरेषु मनोहरेषु
क्वापि प्रयाति सुभगा शरदागमश्रीः ॥ २५॥

* * *

শরতের এই আগমণী শোভা
রমণী বদন কিরণ শশিরে
হংসের নাদ ভারি নিক্কণ
মণিময় তা'র নূপুর ধ্বনিরে
অধর-মাধুরী বন্ধুক আভা
পরম হরষে ধরেছিল নারী
আজিকার দিনে কেন নাহি জানি,
তাহারে সে কোথা যায় সে গো ছাড়ি ! ২৫

* * *

Autumn departs at last, but women's cheeks keep still
The luster of its moons, their jingling anklets fill
The air like choirs of geese and their plump mouths assume
The hue that snared the eye in the *bandhuka* bloom. (25)

বিকচকমলবক্ত্রা ফুল্লনীলোৎপলাক্ষী
বিকসিতনবকাশশ্বেতবাসো বসানা ।
কুমুদরুচিরকান্তিঃ কামিনীবোন্মদেযং
প্রতিদিশতু শরদ্ধশ্বেতসঃ প্রীতিমগ্র্যাম্ ॥ ২৬॥

ইতি শরদ্বর্ণনং নাম তৃতীয়ঃ সর্গঃ ॥

* * *

বিকচ-কমল-বদন যাহার
ফুল্ল-সুনীল-উৎপল আঁখি
বিকশিত নব কাশের কুসুমে
আছে যে তাহার বসনেতে ঢাকি !
কুমুদের রুচি কান্তি সুচারু
ললনার মত যৌবনে মাতি
মনের পরম প্রীতির কারণ
শরৎ রহুক তব প্রিয় সাথী ! ২৬

শরৎবর্ণন সমাপ্ত

* * *

May this fair autumn season, whose bewitching eyes
And smiling face the blossoms in her pools comprise,
Dressed in a fleece of kasha flowers, her silk attire,
Yield to you like a willing girl your heart's desire! (26)

Canto 4
Winter

হেমন্ত—ঋতুসংহার পৃঃ ৩৮

নবপ্রবালোদ্ভ্রমসস্যরম্যঃ
　প্রফুল্ললোধ্রঃ পরিপক্কশালিঃ ।
বিলীনপদ্মঃ প্রপতত্তুষারো
　হেমন্তকালঃ সমুপাগতোঽয়ম্ ॥ ১॥

* * *

হেমন্তকাল সমাগত প্রিয়া
নব-পল্লবে শস্য শ্যামল
পক্ক শালিকা ধান্যেতে ভরা
লোধ্র ফুটিয়া ফুল্ল বিহ্বল !
বিলীন পদ্ম, তুষার পতনে
সুবিমল ভাতি ধরণী ভরিয়া
রমণীয় শোভা অতি মনোলোভা
চারিভিতে আজি আছে গো ধরিয়া । ১

* * *

Now has the barley flowered in every field;
　The *lodhra* tree has gained, the lotus lost
Their blooms; now winter's advent is revealed
　By its delicious days and nights of frost. (1)

मनोहरैश्चन्दनरागगौरैस्
तुषारकुन्देन्दुनिभैश्च हारैः ।
विलासिनीनां स्तनशालिनीनां
नालंक्रियन्ते स्तनमण्डलानि ॥ २॥

* * *

বিলাসিনী সবে পয়োধর ভারে
কুঙ্কুম রাগে রাতুল শোভায়
তুষার-কুন্দ, ইন্দু-হারেতে
বক্ষ-কক্ষে শোভিতেছে তায় ! ২

* * *

As lustrous as the moonbeams, cool and white
    Like snowflakes, precious necklaces of pearls
Are set aside, no longer a delight
    To the soft bosoms of voluptuous girls. (2)

न बाहुयुग्मेषु विलासिनीनां
   प्रयान्ति सङ्गं वलयाङ्गदानि ।
नितम्बबिम्बेषु नवं दुकूलनवं
   तन्वंशुकं पीनपयोधरेषु ॥ ३ ॥

* * *

বালা অঙ্গদ সঙ্গ না লয়
পুরবাসিনীর বাহুযুগ 'পরে
নিতম্ব-তটে নব-উত্তরী
বক্ষে চিকন বসন না ধরে ! ৩

* * *

In wintertime, the bracelet must forsake
   The contact of its mistress' slender arm;
Now garments of the finest silk partake
   No longer of her figure's sensuous charm. (3)

काञ्चीगुणैः काञ्चनरत्नचित्रैर्
 नो भूषयन्ति प्रमदा नितम्बान् ।
न नूपुरैर्हंसरुतं भजद्भिः
 पादाम्बुजान्यम्बुजकान्तिभाञ्जि ॥ ४॥

* * *

স্বর্ণরতনে ভূষিত দুকূল
নিতম্ব দেশে শোভনের তরে
হংস শব্দ ধ্বনিত নূপুর
পদ অম্বুজে শোভিত না করে ! ৪

* * *

Nor any longer does the girdle ride,
 Flashing with jewels, on its usual seat,
Or scintillating anklets ring with pride,
 Singing like geese, the lilies of her feet. (4)

গাত্রাণি কালীয়কচর্চিতানি
সপত্রলেখানি মুখাম্বুজানি ।
শিরাংসি কালাগুরুধূপিতানি
কুর্বন্তি নার্যঃ সুরতোৎসবায় ॥ ৫॥

* * *

মিলনোৎসবে পুরবালা সবে
মাখিয়া গন্ধ কালীয়কটিরে
বদনেতে করে পত্র-রচনা
কালাগুরু দিয়া ধূপ দেয় শিরে ! ৫

* * *

Extending over incense fumes her hair's
    Luxuriance, making her complexion bright
And body fragrant, now a girl prepares
    To ravish in the revels of the night. (5)

रतिश्रमक्षामविपाण्डुवक्त्राः
संप्राप्तहर्षाभ्युदयास्तरुण्यः ।
हसन्ति नोच्चैर्दशनाग्रभिन्नान्
प्रपीड्यमानानधरानवेक्ष्य ॥ ६॥

* * *

লাস্য-বলাস-খেলাতে তরুণী
কৃশ-দুর্ব্বল রহি প্রেম-ভারে
দশন-আহত পীড়িত অধরে
উল্লাসে সুখে হসিতেনা পারে ! ৬

* * *

Tired by her arduous apprenticeship,
    Yet jubilant, today she must refrain
From laughter, pampering her lower lip
    Which, bitten by her lover, throbs with pain. (6)

৪০

দখিন-অনিল ধীরিতে ধীরে
উল্লাসে মুখে হাসিলেন তাঁর।৬

উঠিতে তুষার হলেন অদর্শ্য
শশাঙ্ক রহিলে মনের মাঝে
দেখিলে যত দুঃখের রাশি
শীতলতা তারি শীতনেত্র নয়।৭

অরুণ আসিলেন ধীরেতে ভার
দুয়টি রয়েণ মুসলময় ঠাঁই
প্লৌকি নিমাদ মুখরিত করি
ধীর্তে তারি কোনা জমায়।৮

ফুল্ল বীলোৎপলের শোভিতে
একদায়ু রাশি হাসের দলে
নির্মল কারি পূরিট শীতল
ঘন হইলো সরোবর জলে।৯

पीनस्तनोरःस्थलभागशोभाम्
	आसाद्य तत्पीडनजातखेदः ।
तृणाग्रलग्नैस्तुहिनैः पतद्भिर्
	आक्रन्दतीवोषसि शीतकालः ॥ ७॥

* * *

উষাতে তুষার তৃণের আগায়
	লগন রহিলে মনে হয় ফাঁদে
ফেলেছে বক্ষ পয়োধর মাঝে
	শীতকাল তারি পীড়নেতে কাঁদে ! ৭

* * *

A dewdrop in the dawn, which like a tear
	Slides slowly down a blade of grass, attests
The season's sympathy for the severe
	Ordeals now endured by lovely breasts. (7)

প্রভূতশালিপ্রসবৈশ্বিতানি
মৃগাঙ্গনাযূথবিভূষিতানি ।
মনোহরক্রৌঞ্চনিনাদিতানি
সীমান্তরাণ্যুৎসুকয়ন্তি চেতঃ ॥ ৮ ॥

* * *

প্রচুর শালিকা ধান্যেতে ভরা
ভূষিত রয়েছে মৃগাঙ্গনায়
ক্রৌঞ্চ নিনাদে মুখরিত করি
সীমান্তে তারি বেদনা জাগায় ! ৮

* * *

Pleasant it is to wander here and there
    Among ripe paddy fields, where one may spy
A silent herd of does or hear somewhere
    The plaintive music of the curlew's cry. (8)

প্রফুল্লনীলোৎপলশোভিতানি
সোন্মাদকাদম্ববিভূষিতানি ।
প্রসন্নতোয়ানি সুশীতলানি
সরাংসি চেতাংসি হরন্তি পুংসাম্ ॥ ৯ ॥

* * *

ফুল্ল নীলোৎপলেতে শোভিত
কলনাদে মাতি হংসের দলে
নির্ম্মল বারি পূরিত শীতল
মন হরিলয় সরোবর জলে ! ৯

* * *

And pleasant are the waters, crystal clear
    And chilling to the touch, in ponds and lakes
Where the blue lotus blooms and there appear
    Flocks of the pink flamingo and wild drakes. (9)

पार्कं व्रजन्ती हिमजातशीतैर्
आधूयमाना सततं मरुद्भिः ।
प्रिये प्रियङ्ग प्रियविप्रयुक्ता
विपाण्डुतां याति विलासिनीव ॥ १० ॥

* * *

প্রিয়ঙ্গুলতা তুষারে শীতল
সমীর কাঁপায়ে পরিণত করি
বিরহিনী নারী পাণ্ডু বিভায়
অপরূপ রূপ আছে আজি ধরি ! ১০

* * *

Shuddering in the breezes that descend
    From far snows, the *priyangu* creeper turns
Pale like a woman sobbing without end
    Through lonely months until her love returns. (10)

পুষ্পাসবামোদসুগন্ধিবক্ত্রো
	নিঃশ্বাসবাতৈঃ সুরভীকৃতাঙ্গঃ ।
পরস্পরাঙ্গব্যতিষঙ্গশায়ী
	শেতে জনঃ কামরসানুবিদ্ধঃ ॥ ১১ ॥

* * *

অঙ্গে অঙ্গ জুড়ায় যুগলে
মিলন আবেশে সোহাগে মাতিয়া
পুষ্প-আসবে আমোদিত সুখে
দেহেতে শ্বাসের সুরভিরে নিয়া
শয়ন করিয়া সুখে যায় ঘুম !
এমনি একাল সবাকার তরে
শীতল-পরশ সুখ-অনুরাগ
দেয় আনি চিতে আজি ঘরে ঘরে ! ১১

* * *

Redolent of the scent of floral wine
	Breathed from warm mouths, released into a light
Slumber, the limbs of couples intertwine
	Tenderly in the stillness of the night. (11)

दन्तच्छदैः सव्रणदन्तचिह्नैः
  स्तनैश्च पाण्यग्रकृताभिलेखैः ।
संसूच्यते निर्दयमङ्गनानां
  रतोपभोगो नवयौवनानाम् ॥ १२ ॥

* * *

সোহাগে-নিরিখ অধরেতে ধরি
বুকে ধরি তার প্রেমের বিভায়
নব যুবতীর লীলা-সন্তোষ
এমনি রয়েছে সূচিত সেথায় ! ১২

* * *

Scarlet nail-carvings on a shapely breast,
  The lush lip with an imprint of a tooth –
These marks on vulnerable flesh protest
  Against the roughness of impassioned youth. (12)

কাচিদ্বিভূষয়তি দর্পণসক্তহস্তা
বালাতপেষু বনিতা বদনারবিন্দম্ ।
দন্তচ্ছদং প্রিয়তমেন নিপীতসারং
দন্তাগ্রভিন্নমবকৃষ্য নিরীক্ষিতং চ ॥ ১৩॥

* * *

নব-রবি মৃদু কিরণে তরুণী
বসিয়া করেতে দর্পণ ল'য়ে
বদন-কমল সোহাগের রাগে
অধরে মধুর নিরিখেরে ব'য়ে
স্বামীর আদর চিহ্নেরে হেরি
আনন্দে হারা গরবে মগন !
গণিছে সে তার ভাগ্য সুখের
হেমন্তে হেরে কি শুভ-লগন ! ১৩

* * *

Mirror in hand, at break of day a girl applies
Cosmetics to restore her pretty face and eyes;
Fondling her lip, a casualty of the night's
Pleasures, she views the ravage of her partner's bites. (13)

अन्या प्रकामसुरतश्रमखिन्नदेहा
रात्रिप्रजागरविपाटलनेत्रपद्मा ।
स्रस्तांसदेशलुलिताकुलकेशपाशा
निद्रां प्रयाति मृदुसूर्यकराभितप्ता ॥ १४ ॥

* * *

লাস্য আবেশে ক্লান্ত রমণী
খিন্ন তনুটি মৃদু রবি করে
তপ্ত-শান্ত রয়েছে ঘুমায়ে
স্কন্ধে স্রস্ত কেশপাশ ধরে !
রাতি জাগরণে পাটল বরণ
ধরিয়াছে আঁখি, রমণীয় অতি !
হেমন্তকালে সুখের উদয়ে
এমনি শান্ত সুধীর সে গতি ! ১৪

* * *

Another girl, exhausted by the sleepless hours,
With bleary eyes like petals of pink lotus flowers,
Her drooping shoulders shrouded in disheveled hair,
Is lulled into a slumber by the sunlit air. (14)

নির্মাল্যদাম পরিভুক্তমনোজ্ঞগন্ধং
মূর্ধ্নোঽপনীয় ঘননীলশিরোরুহান্তাঃ ।
পীনোন্নতস্তনভরানতগাত্রযষ্ট্যঃ
কুর্বন্তি কেশরচনামপরাস্তরুণ্যঃ ॥ ১৫॥

* * *

তরুণী রমণী ফুলের মালার
মধুর সুবাসে গত হেরি তার
মুক্ত করিয়া কবরী বাঁধিছে
মনোহর ধরি বক্ষের ভার !
অবনত তনু, ঘন কালো কেশ,
হেরিয়া সবার মনে সুখ আনে !
রুচির সুরতি তাহাতে জাগায়
পরম হরষ ভরি দিয়া প্রাণে ! ১৫

* * *

Tossing aside a wilted garland which has spent
Its fragrance, yet another slender maid, intent
On combing her black, tangled tresses, lifts her arms
And gracefully reveals her bosom's heightened charms. (15)

হেমন্তবরন   ৪১

তরুণী-রমণী সুন্দর সদাগর
মধুর সুবাস সদ পোরি তার
মুখ কমিলা-কবরী সাঁজিত
মদনের ধীরি বধূর ভাঁও। ১৩০
অনন্ত তনু, ঘন কালো কেশ,
ঢৌরিণা আকার ধনে সুখ আনে।
রুচির মুরতি সহসতে আসনে
পরম হরষ ভারি দিয়া গায়।১৩

কদমিনী সে কোমল, শীতল বিরিখ
দ্বিগুণ পরশ সাধ্যমতে ধরি
সুনীত-বালো দিকম চিকুর
অর্ধ-মুদি আঁখ অনায়মন্তভির
প্রিয়জন সত মিতা দেখতে
বৌরেৎ পরম হরষ লাগিয়া
কঙ্কনী পরি আসাজিত গবরে
অতিপলে সব চকমোহ দিয়া।১৬

শ্রী
দ্বাসা১৫

अन्या प्रियेण परिभुक्तमवेक्ष्य गात्रं
हर्षान्विता विरचिताधरचारुशोभा ।
कूर्पासकं परिदधाति नखक्षताङ्गी
व्यालम्बिनीललिताललककुञ्चिताक्षी ॥ १६ ॥

* * *

কামিনী সে কোনো, লীলার নিরিখ
দেহের পরেতে রাখিয়াছে ধরি
লুষ্ঠিত কালো চিকন-চিকুর
আধ-মুদি আঁখি অলসেতে ভরি
প্রিয়জন গত নিজ দেহলতা
হেরিছে পরম হরষ লভিয়া
কঞ্চুলী পরি সাজিহে বাসরে
অধরেতে তার চারুশোভা নিয়া ! ১৬

* * *

Surveying on her luscious figure with a faint
Exultant smile the signs of passion's unrestraint,
One slips into her bodice and her eyes contract
To feel it touch the parts her lover's nails attacked. (16)

अन्याश्चिरं सुरतकेलिपरिश्रमेण
	खेदं गताः प्रशिथिलीकृतगात्रयष्ट्यः ।
संहृष्यमाणपुलकोरुपयोधरान्ता
	अभ्यञ्जनं विदधति प्रमदाः सुशोभाः ॥ १७॥

* * *

শোভনা প্রমদা তৈল সুবাস
মাখিছে অঙ্গে শীতল শোভন
সন্তোষ-সুখ-রভসে শ্রান্ত
শিথিল সে তনু অবসাদ মন,
বক্ষ অন্তে রোমাঞ্চ আনি
চায় ফিরে ফিরে পথিকের পানে
এমন সুখের দিনগুলি হায়
কার না বিমল আনন্দ আনে ?   ১৭

* * *

Others, their fragile bodies wearied by the toil
Of the night's strenuous enjoyments, sprinkle oil
And rub their aching breasts and thighs, where downy hair
Rises erect on contact with the morning air. (17)

बहुगुणरमणीयो योषितां चित्तहारी
परिणतबहुशालिव्याकुलग्रामसीमा ।
विनिपतिततुषारः क्रौञ्चनादोपगीतः
प्रदिशतु हिमयुक्तस्त्वेष कालः सुखं वः ॥ १८ ॥

इति हेमन्तवर्णनं नाम चतुर्थः सर्गः ॥

* * *

বহুগুণে সে যে রমণীয় অতি
অবলাগণের মন লয় হরি
ক্রৌঞ্চমালার শোভায় শোভন
বিবিধ ধান্য গ্রামসীমা ভরি
পরিণত সবি ; হে সখি আমার !
আনন্দ দেয় ব্যথা করি দূর
হেমন্তে সবি পুলক বিকাশি
রেখে যায় তার স্মৃতি সুমধুর ! ১৮

হেমন্তবর্ণন সমাপ্ত

* * *

Season of many beauties, when the fields entice
With calling of the curlews and the nodding rice,
When women are abandoned to their hearts – may this,
The frosty time of winter, shower you with bliss! (18)

Canto 5
Dew-Time

প্ররূঢশালীক্ষুচয়াবৃতক্ষিতিং
ক্বচিত্স্থিতক্রৌঞ্চনিনাদরাজিতম্ ।
প্রকামকামং প্রমদাজনপ্রিয়ং
বরোরু কালং শিশিরাহ্বয়ং শৃণু ॥ ১॥

* * *

তন্বী, শোনো গো ! শিশিরেরকালে
রমণীগণের মন মধু ভরে
পক্ক ধান্যে উজলি ধরণী
হৃদয় সবার বিমোহিত করে !
ক্রৌঞ্চ-নিনাদ ভ'রে দিশিদিশি
শোভা ধরে তায় বিপুল বিভায়
এমন মধুর কালেতে সখি গো,
কতই আমোদে দিন কেটে যায় ! ১

* * *

Verdant with fields of soaring sugarcane,
Melodious with the heron's floating strain,
Dew-time is here, my love, when passions rise
In ardent youths and girls with shapely thighs! (1)

পত্র ও কবিতা

শিশিরবর্ণন

তন্বী, শোনলো তাে! শিশিরের কালে
কামিনীগণের মন মত্ত করে ৩৩
বকুল ঈষল্ উড়ালি ঈষণী - ৩ ত
যাদু সবার বিসাইত করে!২
কোথা- বিনিদ্র ভ'রে দিশি দিশি
শোভা ধরে তায় বিপুল বিডায়
এমন মধুর কালেতে সাধিলে,
কত হ আমাদে দিন কেটে যায়! ১

কুহু ভাবনা হ্য়-মন্দির ৩৩
দুয়ালন ওম, ভানুর কিরণ-,
সকল আর পুরটী-রমণী- ত৩
(এই) সকলয় সকলে সুখেতে জীবন!২
শ্রীঅনাদি

निरुद्धवातायनमन्दिरोदरं
हुताशनो भानुमतो गभस्तयः ।
गुरूणि वासांस्यबलाः सयौवनाः
प्रयान्ति कालेऽत्र जनस्य सेव्यताम् ॥ २॥

* * *

রুদ্ধ জানালা গৃহ-মন্দিরে
হুতাশন তাপ, ভানুর কিরণ,
গুরুবাস আর যুবতী-রমণী
কাটায় সকলে সুখেতে জীবন ! ২

* * *

To sit indoors beside a crackling blaze
Is a good way to pass these chilly days,
The windows closed. Now woollen clothing warms
Or the encirclement of tender arms. (2)

ন চন্দনং চন্দ্রমরীচিশীতলং
    ন হর্ম্যপৃষ্ঠং শরদিন্দুনির্মলম্ ।
ন বায়বঃ সান্দ্রতুষারশীতলা
    জনস্য চিত্তং রময়ন্তি সাম্প্রতম্ ॥ ৩॥

* * *

চন্দ্র-মরীচি, হিম-চন্দন
করেনা হরণ মনেরে এখন
শরৎ ইন্দু-সিত-সৌধেতে
বিহারীতে প্রীতি নাহিক তেমন !
তুষার-আর্দ্র বায়ু সুশীতল
শরীর রসিত করেনাক আর
শীতের পরশে সকলি বিমুখ
ধরে তাতে আজি যেন গুরুভার ! ৩

* * *

Now is the soothing sandal paste enjoyed
No more; the moonlit terrace-floors are void
Of pleasure to the feet, while breezes lose
Their charm when cooled too much by heavy dews. (3)

तुषारसंघातनिपातशीतलाः
    शशाङ्कभाभिः शिशिरीकृताः पनः ।
विपाण्डुतारागणचारुभूषणा
    जनस्य सेव्या न भवन्ति रात्रयः ॥ ४ ॥

* * *

তুষারের ঘাত নিপাত-শীতল
পাণ্ডু তারায় বিমলিন ভাতি
শশাঙ্ক ভ'রে শিশির হিমাণী
না রয় যোগ্য সেবনীয় রাতি ! ৪

* * *

Frigid with condensation of untold
Legions of dewdrops, pallid-hued and cold
With icy moonbeams, night's unkindness mars
Her beauty sumptuous with diamond stars. (4)

गृहीतताम्बूलविलेपनस्रजः
पुष्पासवामोदितवक्त्रपङ्कजाः ।
प्रकामकालागुरुधूपवासितं
विशन्ति शय्यागृहमुत्सुकाः स्त्रियः ॥ ५॥

* * *

সোৎসুকে নারী তাম্বুল, মালা
বদন আসবে, সুখ বিলেপন
কালাগুরু রসে, নিবিড় ধূপেতে
শয়ন ঘরেতে করিছে গমন ! ৫

* * *

A hint of floral liquor on her lips,
Fresh-bathed and garlanded, a woman slips
With quickened heartbeats to her husband's room,
Where incense sticks diffuse a rich perfume. (5)

कृतापराधान्बहुशोऽभितर्जितान्
सवेपथून्साध्वसलुप्तचेतसः ।
निरीक्ष्य भर्तृन्सुरताभिलाषिणः
स्त्रियोऽपराधान्समदा विसस्मरुः ॥ ६ ॥

* * *

কৃত-অপরাধে তর্জ্জিত পতি
ভয়ে সারা কাঁপে নেহারিয়া তারে
আততায়ী তবে, প্রেম অভিলাষী
ভোলে অপরাধ নারী কৃপাধারে ! ৬

* * *

Discovered in their infidelities,
Rebuked and brought repentant to their knees,
Remorseful husbands tremble to receive
From yielding lips an amorous reprieve. (6)

प्रकामकामैर्युवभिः सुनिर्दयं
	निशासु दीर्घास्वभिरामिताश्चिरम् ।
भ्रमन्ति मन्दं श्रमखेदितोरवः
	क्षपावसाने नवयौवनाः स्त्रियः ॥ ७ ॥

* * *

দীঘল রজনী বিলাসী তরুণ
মিলন-বাসরে জাগরণ শ্রমে
রাতি অবসানে যুবতীরা তাই
খেদ মিটাবারে ধীরে ধীরে ভ্রমে ! ৭

* * *

Released at last from exquisite delights
Inflicted through interminable nights
By lusty youths, young women, rising late
With limp thighs, move about with languid gait. (7)

मनोज्ञकूर्पासकपीडितस्तनाः
सरागकौशेयकभूषितोरवः ।
निवेशितान्तःकुसुमैः शिरोरुहैर्
विभूषयन्तीव हिमागमं स्त्रियः ॥ ८ ॥

* * *

রমণীরা কেশ কুসুমে ভরিয়া
শিশির কালেতে রহে সজ্জিত
কঞ্চুকী দেহে করিছে পীড়ন
জঘন রঙিন ভূষণে ভূষিত ! ৮

* * *

Fair creatures with their swelling bosoms pressed
Beneath tight bodices, their thighs caressed
By brightly colored silks and black locks twined
With blossoms, stamp their beauty on the mind. (8)

पयोधरैः कुङ्कुमरागपिञ्जरैः
सुखोपसेव्यैर्नवयौवनोष्मभिः ।
विलासिनीभिः परिपीडितोरसः
स्वपन्ति शीतं परिभूय कामिनः ॥ ९॥

* * *

যৌবন-তাপে তাপিত কামিনী
কুঙ্কুম রাগে পীত শোভা তায়
ক্ষেতে ধরে পতিরে নিবিড়
পীড়নেতে তার শীত দূরে যায় !
সুখেতে তাহারা ঘুমেতে মগন
স্বপন বিভোরে পরম হরষে !
কেটে যায় রাতি এমনি শিশিরে
তপ্ত পেলব অঙ্গ পরশে ! ৯

* * *

Enjoying, squeezed against their throbbing chests,
Their sweet companions' intimate warm breasts
Which leave a glow of saffron, young men glide
To sleep oblivious of the frost outside. (9)

সুগন্ধিনিঃশ্বাসবিকম্পিতোৎপলং
মনোহরং কামরতিপ্রবোধকম্ ।
নিশাসু হৃষ্টাঃ সহ কামিভিঃ স্ত্রিয়ঃ
পিবন্তি মদ্যং মদনীয়মুত্তমম্ ॥ १० ॥

* * *

হরষ-পুলকে কামিনীরা সবে
নিশীথে যাপিছে পতিজন লয়ে,
সুগন্ধিশ্বাস হিলোল-কমলে
জীবন-রসের মাদকতা ব'য়ে
মত্ততা আনি, করে মনহর
পান করি সুখে আসরের মধু
এমনি হরষে শিশিরের রাতি
কাটায় সুখেতে ঘরে ঘরে বধূ ! ১০

* * *

Nestled in loving arms a woman sips,
Disturbing with the fragrance from her lips
The lily in the goblet, potent wine
Whose transports and the surging blood combine. (10)

अपगतमदरागा योषिदेका प्रभाते
कृतनिबिडकुचाग्रा पत्युरालिङ्गनेन ।
प्रियतमपरिभुक्तं वीक्षमाणा स्वदेहं
व्रजति शयनवासाद्वासमन्यं हसन्ती ॥ ११॥

* * *

বধূ বা সে কেহ, স্বামীর সোহাগ
সুখ-ভরা নিজ-দেহ দেখি হাসে
শয়ন ছাড়িয়া যায় আর ঘরে
অপগত-মদ-রাগেতে সে ভাসে !
বুকের কঁচুলি গেছে যে জড়ায়ে
প্রিয়জন নাই এখন যে কাছে !
সুখভরি রহে বিগত রজনী
মিলনের ব্যথা স্মৃতি জাগি আছে ! ১১

* * *

No longer flushed with drink, but ravishingly dressed
In blushing tints of sunrise, nipples still compressed
As she recalls her lover's clasp, a girl admires
With laughing eyes the limbs that thrilled to his desires. (11)

अगुरुसुरभिधूपामोदितं केशपाशं
गलितकुसुममालं कुञ्चिताग्रं वहन्ती ।
त्यजति गुरुनितम्बा निम्ननाभिः सुमध्या
उषसि शयनमन्या कामनी चारुशोभा ॥ १२ ॥

* * *

অগুরু সুরভি ধূপে আমোদিত
কুঞ্চিত কেশ বিস্তারি রহে
গলিত কুসুম মাল্য তাহার
গুরু নিতম্ব, ক্ষীণ-কটি বহে ;
চারুশোভা ধরি চলিয়াছে নারী
শয়ন ত্যজিয়া প্রভাতের কালে
রূপ মনোরম, সুখের দরদ
লেখা যেন আছে তাহাদের ভালে ! ১২ ॥

* * *

Another lifts her beauty from a bed where hours
Of ecstasy have sprinkled an array of flowers
Dislodged from the dense, scented hair whose curly tips
Caress her sunken navel and curvaceous hips. (12)

কনককমলকান্তৈশ্চারতাম্রাধরোষ্ঠৈঃ
শ্রবণতটনিষক্তৈঃ পাটলোপান্তনেত্রৈঃ ।
উষসি বদনবিম্বৈরংসসংসক্তকেশৈঃ
শ্রিয় ইব গৃহমধ্যে সংস্থিতা যোষিতোঽদ্য ॥ ১৩ ॥

* * *

সদ্য স্নানের সুরভি ভরিয়া
কনক-কমল কান্তিরে মাখি
স্কন্দ-লগন কেশ-কলাপেতে
রক্তপ্রান্ত আকীর্ণ আঁখি
বিস্ফারি গৃহে বিহারিছে নারী
লক্ষ্মীরূপিণী প্রভাতে সেথায়
রমণীয় তনু রাতুল চরণে
শিশিরের শীতে কম্পিত কায় ! ১৩

* * *

With faces like gold lotuses and eyes that reach
The ears almost with their red corners, now in each
Fortunate household wives whose tresses flood their arms
Awake like smiles of Lakshmi, goddess of all charms. (13)

पृथुजघनभरार्ताः किंचिदानम्रमध्याः
    स्तनभरपरिखेदान्मन्दमन्दं व्रजन्त्यः ।
सुरतसमयवेषं नैशमाशु प्रहाय
    दधति दिवसयोग्यं वेषमन्यास्तरुण्यः ॥ १४॥

* * *

পৃথু-ঘন তার জঘনের ভার
নত কটি গুরু-বক্ষে বহন
করিয়া নিশার তেয়াগি পরিছে
আশু দিবসের যোগ্য বসন ! ১৪

* * *

The burden of their hips encumbering their gait,
Their waists as if too slight to bear their bosoms' weight,
Young ladies shed the scant apparel of the night
To dress their gorgeous bodies for the day's delight. (14)

नखपदचितभागान्वीक्षमाणाः स्तनान्तान्
   अधरकिसलयाग्रं दन्तभिन्नं स्पृशन्त्यः ।
अभिमतरतवेषं नन्दयन्त्यस्तरुण्यः
   सवितुरुदयकाले भूषयन्त्याननानि ॥ १५॥

* * *

অরুণ উদয়ে তরুণীরা সবে
নিজ নিজ শুভ-নিরিখেরে হেরে
অধর-পত্রে দন্ত-আঘাত
পরশন করি আনন্দে ঘেরে ! ১৫

* * *

The rising sun each day is witness to the art
Of maids who, as they toil before their mirrors, dart
Shy glances at the bite-marks on a tender lip
Or breasts that show a keen-nailed passion's workmanship. (15)

প্রচুরগুডবিকারঃ স্বাদুশালীক্ষুরম্যঃ
    প্রবলসুরতকেলির্জাতকন্দর্পদর্পঃ ।
প্রিয়জনরহিতানাং চিত্তসন্তাপহেতুঃ
    শিশিরসময় এষ শ্রেয়সে বোঽস্তু নিত্যম্ ॥ ১৬ ॥
ইতি শিশিরবর্ণনং নাম পঞ্চমঃ সর্গঃ ॥

* * *

প্রচুর গুড়ের বিকারে ঘটিত
সুস্বাদু ধান, ইক্ষু সুধায়
প্রিয়জন হারা নারীর মনেতে
বিরহ কালে যে সন্তাপ পায়
হরণ করুক ইহারে সেবিয়া
বাসনা কামনা আনে যে শিশিরে
সুখ-মিলনেতে চিত্ত যে ধায়
ভুলাক হে সাথি, পান করি ধীরে ! ১৬

শিশিরবর্ণন সমাপ্ত

* * *

The season of lush fields of sugarcane and rice,
When sweets abound and love-play has an added spice –
But torture to the hearts of parted men and wives –
May Dew-time in its bounty bless your happy lives! (16)

Canto 6
Spring

বসন্ত—ঋতুসংহার পৃঃ ৫২

प्रफुल्लचूताङ्करतीक्ष्णसायको
द्विरेफमालाविलसद्धनुर्गुणः ।
मनांसि भेत्तुं सुरतप्रसङ्गिनां
वसन्तयोद्धा समुपागतः प्रिये ॥ १ ॥

* * *

সুখ-বাসরেতে আসক্ত জনে
বিদ্ধ করিতে যোদ্ধা তরুণ
মধুঋতু আসে সখি হে আমার !
মধুকর মালা ধনুকের গুণ,
বিলসিত রহে ; আম্র মুকুলে
ধরি লয়ে তার তীক্ষ্ণ সায়ক,
অভিভূত তায় ভরি নিতে চায়
তরুণ, তরুণী, নায়িকা, নায়ক ! ১

* * *

The shoots that burst forth on the mango trees
    Are poignant arrows Spring the archer hurls,
Twanging his bowstring in the hum of bees,
    To wound enamored youths and playful girls. (1)

द्रुमाः सपुष्पाः सलिलं सपद्मं
स्त्रियः सकामाः पवनः सुगन्धिः ।
सुखाः प्रदोषा दिवसाश्च रम्याः
सर्वं प्रिये चारुतरं वसन्ते ॥ २॥

* * *

তরু ফুলে ভরা, সলিল কমলে
প্রেম ভরা নারী, বায়ু সুগন্ধে
সুখের প্রদোষে, রম্য দিবসে
সকলি সুচারু আজি বসন্ত ! ২

* * *

Boughs droop with blossoms in the honeyed air;
    Lakes teem with lotuses. Now Spring imparts
His charm to noon and eve and lends a rare
    Enchantment to each beat of youthful hearts. (2)

वापीजलानां मणिमेखलानां
    शशाङ्कभासां प्रमदाजनानाम् ।
चूतद्रुमाणां कुसुमानतानां
    ददाति सौभाग्यमयं वसन्तः ॥ ३॥

* * *

বাপীর নীরেতে জল কেলি তরে
নারী কটিধরে মণি-মেখলায়,
আম্র মুকুলে কানের ভূষণে
শশি কিরণের বিমল আভায়,
পুলকে মগন প্রমদারা এবে
সকলি মধুর মধুকালে রয়
তাই দেখ সবি সুখ-বিহ্বল
বসন্তে হয় ভাগ্য উদয় ! ৩

* * *

The sparkling pools, the girdle's jewelled bands
    That flash once more, the dreaming moon on high,
The flowering mango groves – all these the hands
    Of Spring have made a rapture to the eye. (3)

कुसुम्भरागारुणितैर्दुकूलैर्
नितम्बबिम्बानि विलासिनीनाम् ।
तन्वंशुकैः कुङ्कुमरागगौरैर्
अलङ्क्रियन्ते स्तनमण्डलानि ॥ ४ ॥

* * *

কুসুম্ভ ফুলে বসন রাঙায়ে
সাজি নিতম্বে বিলাসিনীজন
কুঙ্কুম রাগে উত্তরী রাঙি
পীন বক্ষেরে করিছে শোভন ! ৪

* * *

The curves of captivating hips are dressed
    In the silk flame of safflower-tinted robes;
Light upper garments saffron-dyed arrest
    The gaze upon the bosom's perfect globes. (4)

কর্ণেষু যোগ্যং নবকর্ণিকারং
    চলেষু নীলেষ্বলকেষ্বশোকম্।
পুষ্পং চ ফুল্লং নবমল্লিকায়াঃ
    প্রয়ান্তি কান্তিং প্রমদাজনানাম্ ॥ ৫॥

* * *

কানের যোগ্য নব-কর্ণিকা
প্রমদাগণের শুভ-আভরণ
নীল চঞ্চল কেশেতে অশোক
নব মল্লিকা করিছে ধারণ ! ৫

* * *

The scarlet *karnikara* buds are fair,
  But fairer on the ears of pretty girls.
Ashoka flowers and jasmine in the hair
  Are brightened by the darkness of their curls. (5)

स्तनेषु हाराः सितचन्दनार्द्रा
    भुजेषु सङ्गं वलयाङ्गदानि ।
प्रयान्त्यनङ्गातुरमानसानां
    नितम्बिनीनां जघनेषु काञ्च्यः ॥ ६॥

* * *

রঙ্গরসিকা পুরবধূ সবে
জঘনে মেখলা, বক্ষেতে সাজে
শ্বেত চন্দনে চর্চ্চিত হার
বাহুযুগে বালা অঙ্গদ রাজে ! ৬

* * *

Once more the breasts of lovesick beauties yearn
    For the cool touch of pearls and sandal paste.
The bracelets banished from their arms return,
    While girdles swing again below the waist. (6)

सपत्रलेखेषु विलासिनीनां
    वक्त्रेषु हेमाम्बुरुहोपमेषु ।
रत्नान्तरे मौक्तिकसङ्गरम्यः
    स्वेदागमो विस्तरतामुपैति ॥ ७॥

* * *

পত্র-লেখায় কনক-কমল
    বদনেতে ভ'রে কামিনীরা স্বেদ
রতনের মাঝে মুকুতার যোগে
    বিস্তারি শোভে নাহি কোনো খেদ ! ৭

* * *

Today upon the golden cheeks where girls
    Paint arabesques with many-colored dye,
As if assorted gems were mixed with pearls,
    Clear beads of sweat appear and multiply. (7)

उच्छ्वासयन्त्यः श्लथबन्धनानि
गात्राणि कन्दर्पसमाकुलानि ।
समीपवर्तिष्वधुना प्रियेषु
समुत्सुका एव भवन्ति नार्यः ॥ ८ ॥

* * *

বসন্তে নিজ পতি কাছে এলে
মধুমাসে হেন পুলকে শিহরে
বসন শিথিল ভাব-রসে ভরি
অতি সুখে দেহ হরষেতে ভ'রে ! ৮

* * *

Loosening clothes grown suddenly too tight
    To let their bodies breathe, now women turn
Their thoughts to passion, longing to unite
    Utterly with the ones for whom they yearn. (8)

তনূনি পাণ্ডূনি মদালসানি
মুহুর্মুহুর্জৃম্ভণতৎপরাণি ।
অঙ্গান্যনঙ্গঃ প্রমদাজনস্য
করোতি লাবণ্যসসংভ্রমাণি ॥ ৯ ॥

* * *

সুখ-রস-ভাবে প্রমদাজনেরা
পাণ্ডু তন্বী জড়ের মতন
বার বার তায় জৃম্ভন ভরি
শোভা সম্ভ্রমে রয়েছে মগন ! ৯

* * *

Stretching in self-indulgent indolence
    Their pallid limbs, love-smitten maids reveal
In their intoxicated looks a sense
    Of the excitement of their own appeal. (9)

नेत्रेषु लोलो मदिरालसेषु
गण्डेषु पाण्डुः कठिनः स्तनेषु ।
मध्येषु निम्नो जघनेषु पीनः
स्त्रीणामनङ्गो बहुधा स्थितोऽद्य ॥ १० ॥

* * *

অনঙ্গ ধরে রমণী অঙ্গে
গণ্ডে পাংশু, স্তনেতে কঠিন
মদিরা-অলস-রসে আঁখিভরি
মধ্যে নিম্ন জঘনেতে পীন ;
বহুভাগে ভাগ করিয়া নিজেরে
দেখায় আপন শোভার বাহার,
বসন্ত সেনা মধুকালে আসে
উজলি প্রকাশি বিভব তাহার ! ১০

* * *

Charged with love's power, the eyes of women dart
    More languorously; their cheeks of paler gold,
Firm breasts, the curves of waist and hips – each part
    Becomes a fascination to behold. (10)

বসন্তবর্ণন   ৫৬
নাবকর রয় অতুলন ভরি
মাধব মধুরস রযেছ মগন। ।

অনঙ্গ বীরের রমনীর অঙ্গে-
সাজে - সাজ সঙ্গ, শুনতে সঘন
মদিরা-অলস - রসে আঁখিভরি
মন্দ্র নিম্ন জঘনেত পীন;-
বহু ভরসে ভরসা-করিয়া বিজোরে
দেখায় আপন সোহাগ বাহার,
বসন্ত সেনা বহুঁকালে আসে
উতরসিদ্ধকামী।এভর এহার।১০

নিদ্রা অলস বিহ্বলনারী
খরীতৃতসেনা বসন্তজাগে,
বচনে মউও মদ - কোকলেত
মধুর কুহরি-ধীরী অনুরাগে! ।।

अङ्गानि निद्रालसविभ्रमाणि
वाक्यानि किंचिन्मदिरालसानि ।
भ्रूक्षेपजिह्मानि च वीक्षितानि
चकार कामः प्रमदाजनानाम् ॥ ११॥

* * *

নিদ্রা অলস বিভ্রমে নারী
শরীরেতে সেনা বসন্ত জাগে,
বচনে ঈষৎ মদ-লালসেতে
ভূকুটি-কুটিল-দিঠি অনুরাগে ! ১১

* * *

Love lends to graceful movements an allure
    Of dreamy lassitude; his stirrings teach
The brows to arch and eyes to be demure,
    Make lyrical the wine-impeded speech. (11)

प्रियङ्कालीयककुङ्कुमाक्तं
   स्तनेषु गौरेषु विलासिनीभिः ।
आलिप्यते चन्दनमङ्गनाभिर्
   मदालसाभिर्मृगनाभियुक्तम् ॥ १२ ॥

* * *

গৌর বক্ষ কুঙ্কুমে রাঙি
প্রিয়ঙ্গু সাথে কালীয়ক মাখি
মৃগনাভি দিয়া চন্দন লেপি
খুসি অঙ্গনা সুখাবেশে থাকি ! ১২

* * *

A stimulating blend of sandal cream
   With odorous musk and saffron is applied
By artful women to enhance the gleam
   Of breasts where tantalizing charms reside. (12)

गुरूणि वासांसि विहाय तूर्णं
    तनूनि लाक्षारसरञ्जितानि ।
सुगन्धिकालागुरुधूपितानि
    धत्ते जनः काममदालसाङ्गः ॥ १३ ॥

* * *

রঙ্গ-আমোদে অলস অঙ্গ
গুরুবসনেরে ছাড়িয়া ত্বরায়
লাক্ষার রাগে রাঙায়ে ধূপিত
করি লয়ে কালাগুরুর দ্বারায়,
পরি লয়ে পরা চিকন বসন
মধুমাসে হের যুবক সকলে
পুলকে উজলি উৎসাহ ভ'রে
ঋতু উৎসবে চলে দলে দলে ! ১৩

* * *

The garments of the winter are no good
    In springtime; women drape a flimsier dress,
Dyed red, perfumed with smoke of aloeswood,
    On listless limbs warm puffs of air caress. (13)

পুংস্কোকিলশ্চুতরসাসবেন
	মত্তঃ প্রিয়াং চুম্বতি রাগহৃষ্টঃ ।
কূজদ্ দ্বিরফোঽপ্যয়মম্বুজস্থঃ
	প্রিয়ং প্রিয়ায়াঃ প্রকরোতি চাটু ॥ ১৪ ॥

* * *

কোকিল আম্র-রস-মধু পানে
মত্ত হৃষ্ট অনুরাগ ভরে
চুম্বি অধর জানায় সোহাগ
ভ্রমর পশিলে কমল উপরে
গুঞ্জনি উঠি হেরিয়া প্রিয়ারে
মনোরঞ্জন চাটুবাদ দানি
নিজ অপরাধ যেন মানি লয়
এমনি মধুর মধুমাস খানি ! ১৪

* * *

Drunk with the juice of mango blossoms, see
    The cuckoo kiss his mate with eager bill!
Buzzing around the lotuses, a bee
    Hums flatteries that make his partner thrill. (14)

ताम्रप्रवालस्तबकावनम्राश्
चूतद्रुमाः पुष्पितचारुशाखाः ।
कुर्वन्ति कामं पवनावधूताः
पर्युत्सुकं मानसमङ्गनानाम् ॥ १५॥

* * *

প্রবাল-পেলব কিশলয় নত
আম্রতরুর মুকুলেতে দোলে
মলয় পবন কম্পিত রহি
অঙ্গনা মন আনন্দে ভোলে ! ১৫

* * *

The burdened branches of the mango trees,
    Laden with flowers and bending down with throngs
Of copper shoots that quiver in the breeze,
    Disturb with loveliness the heart that longs. (15)

आ मूलतो विद्रुमरागताम्रं
    सपल्लवाः पुष्पचयं दधानाः ।
कुर्वन्त्यशोका हृदयं सशोकं
    निरीक्ष्यमाणा नवयौवनानाम् ॥ १६ ॥

* * *

প্রবাল রাগের তাম্র রঙেতে
আমূল অশোক পুষ্প পাতায়
ধারণ করিয়া যুবক যুবতী
হৃদয়ে তাদের শোক আনে হায় ! ১৬

* * *

Bedecked with coral blooms that touch the skies,
    The burgeoning *ashoka* now appears
In glory. But the "griefless" tree belies
    Its name, compelling wistful eyes to tears. (16)

मत्तद्विरेफपरिचुम्बितचारुपुष्पा
मन्दानिलाकुलितनम्रमृदुप्रवालाः ।
कुर्वन्ति कामिमनसां सहसोत्सुकत्वं
बालातिमुक्तलतिकाः समवेक्ष्यमाणाः ॥ १७॥

* * *

আম্র মুকুল গন্ধে আকুল
ভ্রমর সুধার চুম্বন লয়ে
মন্দ পবন মৃদুল পাতায়
হিল্লোলি তায় যাইতেছে ব'য়ে
মুকুল কলিকা দেখিয়া তাহার
প্রিয়জন মনে প্রেম ভরি উঠি
উৎসাহ আর আনন্দ সুখে
বসন্তে হাসি সদা রয় ফুটি ! ১৭

* * *

Their laughing blossom-faces kissed by thirsty bees,
Their tender foliage ruffled gently by the breeze,
The supple jasmine creepers with their tendrils twined
Around the mango trunks are haunting to the mind. (17)

कान्तामुखद्युतिजुषामचिरोद्गतानां
शोभां परां कुरबकद्रुममञ्जरीणाम् ।
दृष्ट्वा प्रिये सहृदयस्य भवेन्न कस्य
कंदर्पबाणपतनव्यथितं हि चेतः ॥ १८ ॥

* * *

কান্তা মুখের দ্যুতিহারী তার
কুরুবক তরু মঞ্জরী দানে
যে শোভা ধরিয়া চিত্ত ভরিছে
হেরি কার প্রেম ব্যথা নাহি আনে ? ১৮

* * *

The flowers whose clusters crowd the *kuravaka* bough
In radiance match the luster of a woman's brow;
Gazing on them, what spirit suffers not the sting
Of unseen shafts – the subtle archery of Spring? (18)

आदीप्तवह्निसदृशैर्मरुतावधूतैः
सर्वत्र किंशुकवनैः कुसमावनम्रैः ।
सद्यो वसन्तसमयेन समाचितेयं
रक्तांशुकां नववधूरिव भाति भूमिः ॥ १९ ॥

* * *

দীপ্ত পাবক-প্রতিম-পবন
চারিদিকে ধায় কাঁপাইয়া এসে
ফুল-ভারে নত কিংশুক বনে
রক্তাংশুক নব বধূ বেশে
ছড়াইয়া যায় শোভা বিস্তারি
বসন্তকালে ভূমির এ ভাতি
জুড়ায় হেরিয়া রসিকজনেরা
যখন নিকটে সখি রহে সাথী ! ১৯

* * *

Today, when of a sudden the *palasha* bowers
Fill everywhere with brilliant multitudes of flowers
That flutter in the breeze like swaying tongues of fire,
Earth dazzles like a bride in flickering red attire. (19)

কিং কিংশুকৈঃ শুকমুখচ্ছবিভির্ন ভিন্নং
কিং কর্ণিকারকুসুমৈর্ন কৃতং নু দগ্ধম্ ।
যৎ কোকিলঃ পুনরয়ং মধুরৈর্বচোভির্
যূনাং মনঃ সুবদনানিহিতং নিহন্তি ॥ ২০॥

* * *

শুক-চঞ্চুর মতন পলাশ
সুন্দরী বধূ সুখ আলিঙ্গন
যুবক পতির করেনি কি তায়
হৃদয় মথিত মন বিদারণ ?
কর্ণিকা ফুল ফুটিলে তবুও
দগ্ধ করেনি তবে সে কি কভু ?
কোকিল সে কেন কাকলিতে হেন
নিহত সবারে করিতেছে তবু ? ২০

* * *

Pierced by the arched *palasha* bloom as by the prick
Of a bright parrot's beak, tormented to the quick
By *karnikara* flowers like flames, alas! how long
Can the love-stricken heart endure the cuckoo's song? (20)

पुंस्कोकिलैः कलवचोभिरुपात्तहर्षैः
कूजद्भिरुन्मदकलानि वचांसि भृङ्गैः ।
लज्जान्वितं सविनयं हृदयं क्षणेन
पर्याकुलं कुलगृहेऽपि कृतं वधूनाम् ॥ २१ ॥

* * *

পিক কুহু-কল-বচনে জানায়
তাহার মনের পরম প্রীতি
গুঞ্জনে মাতি ভ্রমর অধীর
হৃদয় ব্যাকুল করিতেছে নিতি !
সবিনয়-হৃদি কুলবধূ বালা
লজ্জাবতীরে মাতাইয়া তোলে
বসন্ত সেনা আগমন ক্ষণে
কুল গৃহ পরে হৃদয়টি দোলে ! ২১

* * *

In Spring, when the exultant cuckoo pours his notes
Across the land and through the open window floats
A drunken croon of bees, even high-bred ladies feel
The blood rebel, their poise of chaste decorum reel. (21)

आकम्पयन्कुसुमिताः सहकारशाखाः
विस्तारयन् परभृतस्य वचांसि दिक्षु ।
वायुर्विवाति हृदयानि हरन्नराणां
नीहारपातविगमात्सुभगो वसन्ते ॥ २२॥

* * *

মধুকালে আজি নীহার বিহীন
সুখ-সমীরণ বহি কম্পিত
সহকার শাখে কুসুমে দোলায়ে
কোকিল কূজনে করে আমোদিত ! ২২

* * *

Rioting in the movement of the mango boughs,
Spreading abroad the cuckoo's call, the winds carouse,
Delightful in the season when the dews depart,
Quickening with their warm embrace the throbbing heart. (22)

कुन्दैः सविभ्रमवधूहसितावदातैः
उद्द्योतितान्युपवनानि मनोहराणि ।
चित्तं मुनेरपि हरन्ति निवृत्तरागं
प्रागेव रागमलिनानि मनांसि यूनाम् ॥ २३ ॥

* * *

খুসি-বিহ্বল বধূ হাসি সম
কুন্দ কুসুমে স্মিত উপবন
বৈরাগী-মুনি-চিত্তেরে হরে
রাগ বিমলীন যুবকের মন
পূর্ব্বেই সে যে করিয়া হরণ
নিয়েছে আজিকে বসন্ত মধু
তাহারি যে স্বাদ দিতেছে এখন
এমন দিনেতে তাহাতে যে বধূ ! ২৩

* * *

The pleasure groves, lit up by jasmine fresh and white
Like laughter of flirtatious women, could excite
Reveries of romance in a self-mastered sage –
Much more the mind in youth's impressionable age! (23)

आलम्बिहेमरसनाः स्तनसक्तहाराः
कंदर्पदर्पशिथिलीकृतगात्रयष्ट्यः ।
मासे मधौ मधुरकोकिलभृङ्गनादैर्
नार्यो हरन्ति हृदयं प्रसभं नराणाम् ॥ २४ ॥

* * *

বসন্তে নারী হেম কাঙ্ক্ষিতে
বক্ষে ধরিয়া হারের ভূষণ
কামনায় ভরা শিথিল তনুতে
করিছে সবার মনেরে হরণ ! ২৪

* * *

Pearls clinging to their bosoms, girdles hanging slack
About the hips, their bodies weak with love's attack,
Girls in this time of honey, resonant with bees
And calling cuckoos, do with men as their hearts please. (24)

নানামনোজ্ঞকুসুমদ্রুমভূষিতান্তান্
হৃষ্টান্যপুষ্টনিনদাকুলসানুদেশান্ ।
শৈলেয়জালপরিণদ্ধশিলাতলান্তান্
দৃষ্ট্বা জনঃ ক্ষিতিভৃতো মুদমেতি সর্বঃ ॥ ২৫॥

* * *

মনোজ্ঞ ফুল তরু নানাজাতি
মত্ত কোকিল কাকলির রবে
শিলাজতু রস গন্ধে সেথায়
শিলাময় ভূমি দেখে ভরা সবে
আনন্দে ভ'রি চরাচর হেরি
তরুণ হৃদয়ে মাদকতা আনি
বসন্ত দেয় শুভ পরিচয়
কূজন গন্ধে, গাহি তারি বাণী ! ২৫

* * *

A joy it is to roam among the hills in Spring
Amid a blaze of petals, listening to the ring
Of birdsong echoing from peak to tuneful peak
And resting on rock slabs sweet-smelling lichens streak. (25)

नेत्रे निमीलयति रोदिति याति शोकं
घ्राणं करेण विरुणद्धि विरौति चोच्चैः ।
कान्तावियोगपरिखेदितचित्तवृत्तिर्
दृष्ट्वाऽध्वगः कुसुमितान् सहकारवृक्षान् ॥ २६ ॥

* * *

কান্তা বিরহ খেদ ল'য়ে বুকে
আম্র তরুর কুসুমে নেহারি
নিমিলিত আঁখি রোদনে বিরহী
রুধিছে নাসিকা নিজ হাতে তারি । ২৬

* * *

But when the lonely traveller with a whirling mind
Sees mango boughs in splendid flower, his eyes grow blind
With weeping and he blocks his nostrils with his hand
Against the siege of fragrance wafting through the land. (26)

समदमधुकराणां कोकिलानां च नादै:
कुसुमितसहकारै: कर्णिकारैश्च रम्यः ।
इषुभिरिव सुतीक्ष्णैर्मानसं मानिनीनां
तुदति कुसुममासो मन्मथोद्दीपनाय ॥ २७॥

* * *

মদ-উন্মাদ মধুকর আর
কোকিল কূজন মধুর নিনাদে
সহকার তরু কুসুমের শোভা
কর্ণিকা ভরি সুগন্ধ স্বাদে
রম্য বিতানে কুসুম মাসেতে
তীক্ষ্ণ সায়ক মনে যেন হয়
মালিনীর মন উতলা করিয়া
বসন্তে আজি মধুবায়ু বয় ! ২৭

* * *

The love-call of the cuckoo and the drone of bees,
The mango blooms, the flaming *karnikara* trees –
With volleys of such shafts the season overpowers
The pride of wilful women in the month of flowers. (27)

আম্রী মঞ্জলমঞ্জরী বরশরঃ সত্কিংশুকং যদ্ধনুর্
ज्या यस्यालिकुलं कलङ्करहितं छत्रं सितांशुः सितम् ।
মত্তেভো মলয়ানিলঃ পরভৃতা যদ্বন্দিনো লোকজিত্
সোऽয়ং বো বিতরীতরীতু বিতনুর্ভদ্রং বসন্তান্বিতঃ ॥ ২৮ ॥

ইতি বসন্তবর্ণনং নাম ষষ্ঠঃ সর্গঃ ॥

* * *

মঞ্জুল চূত-মঞ্জরী শর,
কিংশুক ফুল ধনুক যাহার
জ্যা আরোপিয়া অলিকুল ধায়
কলঙ্কহীন শশি ছাতা তায় ;
মলয় অনিল মত্ত গজটি
বন্দনা করে কোকিল কূজন
বসন্ত সখা অনঙ্গ দেব
করুন তোমারে সুখ বিতরণ ! ২৮

ঋতুসংহার সমাপ্ত

Astride his elephant in rut,
    The sandal-scented southern breeze,
And wielding a *palasha* bow
    That murmurs with its string of bees,
His quiver filled with mango shoots,
    The moon his parasol of state,
With Spring for minister, his bards
    The cuckoos who in song relate
His godlike deeds – may Love in his world-conquering might
Bestow on you his utter sweetness and delight! (28)

International Publications

Auroville Architecture
by Franz Fassbender

Auroville Form Style and Design
by Franz Fassbender

Landscapes and Gardens of Auroville
by Franz Fassbender

Inauguration of Auroville
by Franz Fassbender

Auroville in a Nutshell
by Tim Wrey

Death doesn't exist
The Mother on Death, Sri Aurobindo on Rebirth
Compiled by Franz Fassbender

Divine Love
Compiled by Franz Fassbender

Five Dream
by Sri Aurobindo

Vision
Compiled by Franz Fassbender

Passage to More than India
by Dick Batstone

The Mother on Japan
Compiled by Franz Fassbender

Children of Change: A Spiritual Pilgrimage
by Amrit (Howard Shoji Iriyama)

Memories of Auroville - told by early Aurovilians
by Janet Feran

The Journeying Years
by Dianna Bowler

Auroville Reflected
by Bindu Mohanty

Finding the Psychic Being
by Loretta Shartsis

The Teachings of Flowers
The Life and Work of the Mother of the Sri Aurobindo Ashram
by Loretta Shartsis

The Supramental Transformation
by Loretta Shartsis

The Mother's Yoga - 1956-1973 (English & Frech)
Vol. 1, 1956-1967 & Vol. 2, 1968-1973
by Loretta Shartsis

Antithesis of Yoga
by Jocelyn Janaka

Bougainvilleas PROTECTION
by Narad (Richard Eggenberger), Nilisha Mehta

Crossroad The New Humanity
by Paulette Hadnagy

Die Praxis Des Integralen Yoga
By M. P. Pandit

The Way of the Sunlit Path
William Sullivan

Wildlife great and small of India's Coromandel
by Tim Wrey

A New Education With A Soul
Marguerite Smithwhite

Featured Titles

Divine Love

The texts presented in this book are selected from the Mother and Sri Aurobindo.

"Awakened to the meaning of my heart. That to feel love and oneness is to live. And this the magic of our golden change, is all the truth I know or seek, O sage."

Sri Aurobindo, Savitri, Book XII, Epilog

A Vision by the Mother

On 28th May 1958, the Mother recounted a vision she once had of a wonderful Being of Love and Consciousness, emanated from the Supreme Origin and projected directly into the Inconscient so that the creation would gradually awaken to the Supramental Consciousness. The Mother's account of this vision was brought out a first time in November 1906, in the Revue Cosmique, a monthly review published in Paris.

A Dream – Aims and Ideals of Auroville
the Mother on Auroville

50 years of Auroville from 28.02.1968 - 28.02.2018

Today, information about Auroville is abundant. Many people try to make meaning out of Auroville – about its conception, to what direction should we grow towards, and, what are we doing here?

But what was Mother's original Dream and what was her Vision for Auroville back then?

Matrimandir Talks by the Mother

This book presents most of Mother's Matrimandir talks, including how she conceived the idea for this special concentration and meditation building in Auroville.

Memories of Auroville - Told by early Aurovilians

Memories of Auroville is a book about the very early days of Auroville based on interviews made in 1997 with Aurovilians who lived here between 1968 and 1973. The interviews presented in this book are part of a history program for newcomers that I had created with my friend, Philip Melville in 1997. The plan was to divide Auroville's history into different eras and then interview Aurovilians according to their area of knowledge. Our first section would cover the years from 1968 till 1973 when the Mother was still in her physical body.

The Way of the Sunlit Path

May The Way of the Sunlit Path be a convenient guide for activating this ancient truth as a support for a Conscious Evolution.
May it illumine the transformation offered to us in the Integral Yoga.

A Dream Takes Shape (in English, French, Hindi)

A comprehensive brochure on the international township of Auroville in, ranging from its Charter and "Why Auroville?" to the plan of the township, the central Matrimandir, the national pavilions and residences, to working groups, the economy, making visits, how to join, its relationship to the Sri Aurobindo Ashram, and its key role in the future of the world. This brochure endeavours to highlight how The Mother envisioned Auroville from its inception, some of the major achievements realised over the years, and some of the difficulties currently faced in implementing the guidelines which she gave.

Mother on Japan

I had everything to learn in Japan. For four years, from an artistic point of view, I lived from wonder to wonder. And everything in this city, in this country, from beginning to end, gives you the impression of impermanence, of the unexpected, the exceptional... ...everything in this city, in this country, from beginning to end, gives you the impression of impermanence, of the unexpected, the exceptional. You always come to things you did not expect; you want to find them again and they are lost – they have made something else which is equally charming.

Auroville Reflected

On 28 February 1968, on an impoverished plateau on the Coromandel Coast of South India, about 4,000 people from around the world gathered for a most unusual inauguration. Handfuls of soil from the countries of the world were mixed together as a symbol of human unity. Why did Indira Gandhi, the erstwhile Prime Minister of India, support this development for "a city the earth needs?" Why did UNESCO endorse this project? Why does the Dalai Lama continue to be involved in the project? What led anthropologist Margaret Mead to insist that records must be kept of its progress? Why did both historian William Irwin Thompson and United Nations representative Robert Muller note that this social experiment may be a breakthrough for humanity even as critics commented, "it is an impossible dream"?

A House For the Third Millennium
Essays on Matrimandir

Nightwatch at the Matrimandir...
A cosmic spectacle; the black expanse above, the big black crater of Matrimandir's excavation carved deep into the soil. The four pillars - two of which are completed and the other two nearing completion - are four huge ships coming together from the four corners of the earth to meet at this pro propitious spot...

Passage to More than India

This book is a voyage of discovery. In 1959 the author, Dick Batstone, a classically educated bookseller in England, with a Christian background, comes across a life of the great Indian polymath Sri Aurobindo, though a series of apparently fortuitous circumstances. A meeting in Durham, England, leads him to a determination to get to the Sri Aurobindo Ashram in Pondicherry, a former French territory south of Madras.